Dear Adrianne,

Much

ABRACADABRA

A Book of Magical Wisdom

LORI BARBARIA

♡ Lori Barbaria

Welcome to The Abracadabra Series . . .

I dedicate this book to sparking the passion of all beings.

May You Experience Infinite Magic!

Abracadabra in Aramaic means, "*I CREATE AS I SPEAK.*"
In Hebrew, avar k'davar means, "It will be according to what
is spoken." In the 2nd century during the Roman Empire,
one suffering from harm, troubles, or disease would wear an
amulet containing the word *Abracadabra.* It was written in
the symbol of an upside-down triangle, which denoted the
idea that as the letters fell away to the point at the bottom, it
would bring the release of all difficulties . . .

A B R A C A D A B R A
A B R A C A D A B R
A B R A C A D A B
A B R A C A D A
A B R A C A D
A B R A C A
A B R A C
A B R A
A B R
A B
A

CONTENTS

Introduction

From The Inside Out . . .

1

Our Spark

A Magical Energy Field

5

The Target

Create Your Reality

33

A Leap Of Faith

Affirmations of the Soul

55

Fear-Less-Ness

The Hero's Journey

73

Transformation

Our Evolution

95

Our Authenticity

The Naked Truth

107

Forgiveness

Our Amnesty

121

Love Rules

Our Heart's Seal

137

Great-full-ness

Our Soul's Delight

147

Power-Full

Superheroes in Human Form

161

The Miracle Zone

Our Magic

185

Abracadabra

Our Alchemy

199

Acknowledgments

213

From The Inside Out . . .

This is a commentary on a way of being that goes against the grain of most of what you have ever commonly learned. It's about unlearning, disremembering, and obliterating all the rules you have previously bought into. It's about stepping off the line and going out of bounds to where the concepts of safe and careful are no longer necessary shelters.

Our innate wisdom is hardwired to shift our being into remembering that we are made of magic. It is time for a refill of the sparked inherent prescription of miraculous consciousness that will activate the powerful sanctity of our magnetism. The course of this journey brings you to look through the keyhole and dive into a world of possibilities where your passport is your imagination and your ticket is your passion. Like Alice in the great Wonderland, we have to let go of all that we think we know and get really modest to get through this keyhole. In the enchanted modern forest of all that exists, the only real bag of tricks we have is to use our inventive resource of awareness and trust to recover the dreams that are being gifted to us. The trick around receiving these gifts is that we can't hold onto them, we must flood the world with them and only then will their endowments benefit us.

The universe, our partner in this dance, likes to swing us around to unbuckle our perceptions and loosen our concepts. The only thing one can do in a state of wonder is to tap into the reality that is instilled with magic and reinvent ourselves from there. This endowment of magic is our source of being—it's embedded in our cells, in our brainwaves, and in our consciousness, as a light field. This light field, which has been photographed with Kirlian photography, shows the flash of electrical discharge that an object has in an electromagnetic field. All living beings have a voltage source with an energy flow, which has a magnetic attraction that draws like kind energy back to itself. This light field charges what we believe, dream, and love, into our reality.

Our inspiration holds the pen, our passions are the ink and we are all artists and wizards who are busy manifesting our creations. As we begin to believe in what sparks us, as opposed to what we are witnessing, our inner world comes online and opens doors to new pathways for us to walk upon. It may sound like a lot of rigmarole that we could just alter our reality by dreaming up a new one, divergently we've been trained to stop daydreaming and snap out of it. Now, snap back into the internal magic that is sparked inside your soul and let it do its thing—it knows exactly what to do. Magic does not have to be manipulated or performed; it's an energy field—just feel for it.

The fact is that our minds simulate the make-believe into a materialized certitude and everyday we bewitch the abstract into actuality. In the bigger picture, we wonder what we could offer to stop destruction, wars, intolerance, pollution, and even save the world? If we take the responsibility to affect just even the space that we encompass then the quality of our succinct energy field is our offering. What we do, think, and feel, absolutely makes a difference. We affect the counterbalance of the expanse we encounter by taking our consciousness higher. A high-minded shift in one's perception shifts the actual world!

It is said in the proponents of the *Chaos Theory*, that a butterfly flapping its wings on one continent can affect the weather on another continent. In the same way that one raindrop raises the level of the ocean, what we do matters. Therefore our every action, thought, and vision counts.

Use this book as a road map to travel into the land of your enchantments and stake a claim on your real fortune. The first step is to imagine our way—the second step is to believe it!

Our Spark
A Magical Energy Field

"Without wonder and insight, acting is just a trade. With it, it becomes creation." – Bette Davis

Who do you think you are? Whoever, whatever, you have decided to be, you are so much magnanimously more than that. You are a creation, acting on the world stage, trying out different roles. Beyond that you are a magical being who came to earth to play in this field of wonder. Beyond that, inside you resides your magical spark that conceptualizes creation. This spark is a potent seed that explodes with life force and has an enormous source of grand abundance. You just forgot.

On a day that I was worrying about my future, I came upon a homeless man sitting on the sidewalk with a dog. He had very kind eyes that drew me in and I emptied out my wallet into his cup. In that moment, I cared less about my future as all I wanted was for this man to be able to feed himself and his dog. I had no idea of the story behind the man, nor, did I need to. There was a connection that pulled me to step away from myself, a reminder that stories are not solid. As I walked on, I realized, that this man's presence was a gift that had shifted me. The next thought I had was that I knew I would always be okay and I felt blessed. To believe oneself as blessed no matter what changes the dynamic of everything that goes on in the sense that all things become a gift. This kind of consciousness wakes us up from all the stories our minds make up that keep us removed from the spark of who we really are. It reminds us that we are powerful beings who can transgress beyond what takes us down, breaks our hearts, and rocks our worlds, because we came here to do exactly that.

There are multiple fields of magic in the everyday world. A flow from one person's kindness travels; it creates a dynamic of generosity. It is natural for such a stream of energy to connect to similar energy; energy is contagious and creates more of the same as it multiplies. We are certainly affected by the energy around us and depending upon our balance we may be pulled under its influence. That homeless man was holding a divine state in his heart, which connected to my heart and activated so much love and compassion that I immediately dropped the story of fear and anxiety. When one energy field uplifts another energy field, it empowers the lower energy field to rise up because a brightened energy field inspires all that comes into contact with it. Therefore a spark of energy holds a potent charged dose of light-filled creative power that is useable. Once a spark resonates within your heart things begin to shift because sparks create new beginnings. Every aspect of our being is charged and upgraded by what sparks for us, so nothing can stay the same. Our intellect is sparked by magnanimous thoughts, which spark ideas, which move, they build up mass and gain momentum to fly. When a connection is sourced, this lively spark morphs into multiple fields and resembling a cell, it splits, regenerates, and sparks even more.

The caveat is that we have to be aware of what we are sparking because in the sense that we are human, we deal with darkness. Our shadow is like a living double with a different perspective on the greater whole of our life; this shadow side has its own agenda. By focusing our consciousness upon our shadow aspect we bring our light there to acknowledge what is going on. Once focused upon, this shady persona just needs consideration and then to be brought back into balance. So question everything, don't be afraid to explore the deeper caves of your dark feelings, there is still potent energy available there to be used, confront this aspect of yourself and demand that your shadow side kneel to your creativity. There is nothing that cannot be interchanged.

Since even questions have energy fields, come up with ones that have the power to ignite scintillating insights, questions that create transformation—questions that have a spark. Question what drives you to conduct yourself in certain ways. Question the meaning for your existence. A potent question draws you closer to yourself as there is no one else out there with the answer. In fact, the answer is not important compared to the question. In many ways, the question is the answer. So question if there are really limits to anything and what is beyond a story, a reality, a world, a cosmos, an eternity. Think about your most important question, use it to define who you are and for the time being be that. Then let it go and be something else: be flexible, be wondrous, and get lost in the activities of your super-consciousness. The activity of billions of cells, breaths, thoughts, dreams, and stories, all affect our existence.

An artist, after many years of struggling, becomes famous. His art is being written about everywhere. He tells me that it's good that his art has exploded but that no one is buying it. He then goes on to tell me how hard it is for artists to make a living. This is a collective story that this fellow believes and will defend. As a result this story will hold him in lockdown until he sparks another story. We can't talk someone out of their story only they can do that. All we can do is break out of our own stories, crack the shell of our old paradigms, and jump off the edge into a new story.

Can we go into the realm of unknowing and be in awe? Can we bypass assumptions, interact with energy fields and transform them for good? Can we travel with our imagination and play with the ideas we find there? These are great questions! Whatever exists between you and a story that stops your evolution is just another story with baggage. Can we participate in more than one story at the same time? Our inner state and our outer realities are often a dual existence—a double life. Our inner world is the authentic reality of who we really are, while outwardly we are busy establishing ourselves in another story—playing with that reality. The outer world is flimsy; we cannot count on things as they appear to be, while any and all assumptions based on surface appearances are just constructed stories supported by a collective consciousness, which we have the option to choose to agree or not.

One might think the logical difference between a homeless person and a billionaire is that one has let his spark go out. We only know what we assume, and by dropping all assumptions we'd not judge a homeless man as unworthy or consider the billionaire a better man because by surmising, we are investing energy in a constructed story, not real truth. In truth, the homeless man could easily be a saint sitting on the sidewalk bestowing blessings on all who pass, while the billionaire conducts himself just like Ebenezer Scrooge. In today's world, Jesus might have looked like a homeless person. The fellow dancing in front of you on the subway could possibly be a descendant of the great Buddha. The gas station attendant might be a man who saves your life; a stranger might be your worst enemy. Your hairstylist could be one of your most potent healers and all the pets living in a one-block radius of your home could be raising everyone's spirits and holding up the light for your entire community.

The best stories are a mystery as what's really going on could be so far out, so potent with magic, so animated with adventure, and so beyond what a human brain can conceive of that it can't be analyzed or proven. We can't really know the state of people's affairs or what the true nature of their identity is. Nor, can we really ever understand the reasoning behind all the madness that exists in this world. Maybe we think if we understand the madness, we can stop it. In actuality, all we can do is stop it in ourselves. To be here in human form is to deal with balancing the dichotomies. What if most of the exterior stories didn't really matter? What if we are playing out a very evolved story for reasons we don't understand?

On another note, what if our need to strive was replaced by a state of allowing and this allowed us to be complete? What if we decided to exist just for the sake of existing? Can we have total trust in the process we're moving through? If we could, then we would not need to deny duality, as we would understand the struggle as being part of the journey, and the great resistance would no longer be such a big deal. This lifetime is our hero's journey, which is about retrieving our spirit and honoring our vital humanness. When these two aspects are in union, the melding of these forces completes us. By this very nature, we don't have to do or be anything else—we just are.

The qualification of a sparked state is that it sets our hearts on fire. The qualification for a higher state of being is to not be lost in low-level stories, emotions, and activities that are empowered with darkness. Yes, dark situations exist and sucker punch the air out of us, they break our hearts, and yet they empower us to keep going because the survival aspect and the mystery are more important than falling apart. As the clouds cross the sun, the sun does not have a fit and destroy them, she waits till they pass, because she is the sun and her only job is to shine. A broken heart is like a broken perfume bottle, amidst the shards of glass, the potent fragrance still exists.

Can we make light of ourselves? Can we grab ourselves back from reactions, knowing that to feel is sublime enough? Can we live as if there was magic in everything including rejection and difficulties? If these questions resonate, then you are in the act of enlightening yourself.

Our spirits have arrived into this dimension on the tails of celestial comets and have come into our exact human form fueled by our original spark. These sparks are made of the same light as stars and their mission is to navigate our paths back towards our primordial enlightenment. We have come from the exact enlightenment we are seeking and so instead of seeking, we must be retrieving. If our enlightenment already fully exists, then we must recognize it while still playing out our roles in the everyday stories we've designed. For instance, I wake up, the cat is meowing, I remember where I am, who I am in this lifetime, what is going on. I sleepily walk to the kitchen and open the cat food can, mechanically feeding the cat. I look out the window to see a beam of sunlight hitting a circle of grass. I connect into the realization that there is another world in that circle of light hitting the grass, seeds are gestating, insects are digging into the earth, and squirrels are running through the circle. Traveling into that other world, there's a brief momentary realization that many worlds exist simultaneously and I am connected into all of them. This is enlightenment. I then feed the cat and wonder who the cat really is. I remember the cat is a spark of love, another gift in my life, and that I have to take out the garbage because it smells. This is functioning in duality.

If many worlds exist, can we be in our story and at the same time be part of other stories? When we are asleep, on another level we could be off somewhere in a very high state of sparked consciousness working things out. Connected into these resonations we access all that we need to survive. When we dream, we are being downloaded with pertinent information along with a dose of vitality with healing upgrades to maintain our presence here. In as much as we are in tune with the intelligence coming in, it supports our existence here. Therefore what happens on the subliminal plane is as potent as what is happening on the physical plane, even more potent.

In the act of imagining and visualizing, we are tapping into subliminal astral planes and then using the gifts we find there to program the energetic matrix around us with ideas. It is a play of consciousness to honor our visions as if they already exist in real time; this sanctions them to catch up into our reality. Contiguous to holding a sparked state, even when we are confronted with facts, reasoning, an explanation, and a law of averages, we are being asked to decide whether we want to go along with the status quo or what our soul needs. We must decide if we will invest in a collective story, stay in our old stories, or if in partnership with our spiritual quintessence we will create the real story of the secret self.

The great universe is constantly prodding us to connect, find the treasure and use the gift. A friend told me she sees it as the universe winking at her. The universe is telling us that something is going to shift when reactionary things happen; we are just crossing paths with what agitates us and accelerates reactions that precipitate change. I call it catalysts of change. A catalyst will push us beyond all that appears to be solid, fixed, known, and comfortable. These turbulent stories drive us to grow faster; they are like plant food, which boosts us to reach higher towards the light even when the air is polluted and it's so overcast the sun appears to be gone. To identify with who we are beyond all things is to tap into a state of consciousness that is beyond form; an awakened state that encapsulates everything that impassions us. When we delve into this state, we move beyond all concepts, ideas, and mindsets, to profoundly witness the many facets of ourselves. Yet like the seasons, who we decide we are, and everything going on around us, is naturally constantly changing. What is amazing is that we can create ourselves as anyone or anything or we could just sit and see what comes.

When it comes down to it, "true identities" and "facades" are both interesting tales that are in play, because this is basically what we are doing in this life—playing. As children, play was our most important activity, though suddenly we were expected to grow up and take our responsibilities seriously, sometimes even considering them matters of life and death. However, to live without amusement should no longer be an option for any of us. After we've become bored with storylines, we have the option to go back to playing so we can try on new roles, personifications, and step into unfamiliar performances. We try-out the safe and timid ones, hide in the secret ones, act out the wild outlandish ones, and brace for the daring ones to see if they fit. In the meantime, when we are stuck and rotating around an issue that seems to be holding us in lockdown, we are getting poked, tapped on the shoulder, and reminded that we need to get back to the garden.

Where is this coming from? It's coming from our highest source—our souls calling. In the garden we find our true nature, we divine on beauty, and cultivate our dreams. We gestate ideas and plant our seeds. The garden is our own energy field, which holds our magic. As far out as we go to pursue the exploration of our exceptional capacities is as greathearted and magical that our reality will become.

Albert Einstein followed an abstract notion when he was working on his theory of relativity. He was asking questions about gravity and the concept of an expanding universe, his theories became equations that could be proven. We are doing is the same by proving to ourselves what is valid for us. The modem of genius lies in expanding our psyche beyond the common humdrum boundaries of a collective consciousness. Thereupon, we are stepping out of a tick-tock reality into our own-sparked reality, which brings us to live in an elated state in the midst of it all. Elated states tap into genius.

Can you fathom that we are not in this game of life alone? Can you consider that otherworldly guardians are our advocates, our true family, our inner circle, and part of our spiritual bloodline that supports us? I have heard my grandmother's words of wisdom in odd needed moments and I can tell you it was not a memory as I felt her spirit right there next to me. I am constantly receiving scintillating realizations that come from other dimensions. An awareness many times arrives in a serendipitous occurrence, in statements heard inside that are not our own, and in dreams. These messages are worthy and come directly from the connections we have in spirit. We are surrounded by guides, talk to them and you will get answers, they are not only in other dimensions, they are right here. Potent messages and meanings are everywhere; still we cannot see them when we are not looking. There are sparkling diamonds in plain view on our path, so focus and begin to see them.

I stepped over a turtle on my morning walk thinking it was an odd-looking rock. On my way back, the turtle was waiting for me with its head poked out, staring at me. To Native Americans, the turtle symbolizes eternal ancient Earth wisdom. The turtle is a being that is very close to the earth and has the ability to be grounded no matter what is happening. When we can interpret messages from animal wisdom, we are literally receiving a download of intelligence. The message I was hearing was to slow down. I was moving too fast and had lost my awareness and the sense of my surroundings. Our determination and persistence will work against us if we cannot pace ourselves to be in sync with the world around us.

Turtles represent beings who are very aware of their surroundings, they know exactly where they are, where they want to go and most importantly when to pull inside. They can teach us about a phenomenon known as inattention blindness—not seeing what is actually there. We must move beyond merely opening our eyes, to open our minds to view the authentic matrix where our eternal wisdom lives. Like turtles, there are times we must tuck deep inside ourselves to go the source of where our magic exists. Once there, we can tap into our zone of omnipotent power, the fertile ground that can transform what is abstract into what is tangible. Our conversations beyond normal reasoning download pertinent inspirations, which invigorate us to shift. The act of shifting is about letting go of one thing for another—we transfer our investment of energy towards new ideas. When we allow our elevated energy to move us, it doesn't matter where it takes us; all that matters is that we are moving. We are just re-patterning our conscious awareness. Experts say that it takes 21 days to form new neural pathways and rewire our programming. If we want more abundance then we must cut the channels on all our hardwired thoughts that believe otherwise. In the aftermath, when the old pattern tries to reattach itself, remind yourself that you've installed a new program.

On this hero's journey we have to hold our own, especially in the sense that our actions and reactions are what will support us in feeling good about ourselves. Heroes follow the force of their own true nature, they understand discomfort as being a part of what is unfolding. They do not step away when strong emotions arise and they don't shut them off, in fact they dive deep down into them because they are not afraid to see what is there. If we're wrestling with anxiety, then our inner heroine needs to get into the snake pit with it to see that it's not real. Maybe we might sob over the shock that there is no turning back, that we can't get lost, go unconscious, or find an escape because we are being called forth to do what we came here to do—give birth to ourselves.

An opportunist understands that there is wealth in all experiences so they don't get stuck in any one place. They continue on knowing there is treasure in what exists. A friend was feeling troubled and asked me to sit with him and just listen. He didn't want to be fixed and he didn't want me to talk him out of his feelings. He knew he was O.K. even though he felt awful. He also knew his story was going somewhere important and that the turbulence was part of the journey. He could feel the power of something inside him being undone, while something new was coming into being. He trusted the shift and even through the difficulty, he could still see the magnificence of what the outcome would be.

Our perceptions expand in moments of awakened consciousness, things are unset from stone, patterns are broken and we are released. I was having a conversation with a friend who was stuck.

I said, "These peaches are luscious, taste one."

She heard, "You are fat and should only eat fruit."

Her response was, "You think I need to be on a diet?"

I then explained to her that what she was doing was just conversing with her own silly storyline and that she needed to go beyond it as it was coloring her world when she could be enjoying a peach with me. In that moment, her consciousness awakened, she saw the truth and instead of defending an old way of being, just in the fact that she saw this silly old perception she was holding, it liberated her. We then enjoyed the peaches together.

Our spark is our life force that is aligned with the power that created us. It was a sparked gravitational pull that brought us into this world along with the same-sparked essence that will carry us off when we go. This spark is our innate divinity, which expands into the fuel from which we create. It is in the hand that holds the pen, the violin bow, or the potter's wheel. This spark is in our fingers when we paint, it's in the reverie of our dreams when we imagine, and in our feet when they dance out these dreams. It is the spark in our heart that cries out when all is not right, a spark that heals our broken heart, a spark that illuminates the thought that we have to leave and start again, and the spark that absolves our tears when we're forgiven. Sparks, like stars, are not one-pointed but emit from all directions, they leap and twirl enticing us to follow them. Sometimes they take us to some very strange destinations as they go where they need, to do what needs to be done. They can be explosive and cause confrontations when they are geared to wake us up. Creating a snap, crackle and a pop, a spark is a faculty member of the unpredictable club, which teaches us how to be certain beyond uncertainty—they rearrange us like an anagram allied with alchemy, which transmutes a common substance into gold. Many times when they are turbulent, what they are doing is unraveling our knots and setting us free.

In a magical reality, the unknown is what makes the adventure. The line between the known and unknown is a thin veil, a double-entendre in the sense that two dynamics are constantly changing places and in the enigma of this we must do the same to be in tandem. We must loosen up to get beyond the riddles by using them to get back to why we were inspired in the first place. To understand the oracular wisdom of the universe is to know that: strangers, animals, all situations, our emotions, our reality, and our dreams, are all our instructors. We are constantly receiving non-stop uncensored messages holding potent information for us to advance from; we just need to translate them. On a sparked journey, there can be sharp turns with many twists, though we shouldn't judge any of it because the spark is in control not us. When we understand this then everything matters and must be considered as part of the whole.

Our spark wakes up the visionary within that is attracted to the highest resonance in the vicinity and knows how to use it. We use it to create the most paramount outcome where the real groove is not really about the end result, getting the money, the lover, or the great success. The real groove is about owning the feeling of completeness and fulfillment that we want in the aftermath—right now. Merging with this feeling makes it a magnetic accomplice that creates more of the same. On a creative roll, a sparked innovative inner thunderstorm speeds up the molecules we're made of. These supercharged notions have a life of their own and this life force goes to work on manifesting our creations even as we sleep. Like a domino effect, one thing triggers the next, as our worldly and spiritual goods leave sparked prospects of themselves on the trail for us to find them. So a spark might not be real in a material sense, but nevertheless a spark has the potency to lead us to what is absolutely viable—if we follow it.

We are being pushed and pulled in all directions, so we must feel our way; our most virtuous bearings have a pull. It's time to follow our true force, and while our inner witness identifies the unaccountability of our rational thinking, our creative genius has gone off to work in the studio and is busy painting our dreams. We must wait for our creative genius to surface because we're all in this together, so if destiny has a role in our game of life, then so does creation, they're both aligned in a totally magnificent synthesized harmonious partnership. Here is their story . . .

Creation and Destiny met and fell in love. Destiny was a bit bossy and kept trying to lead Creation everywhere they went. However, Creation could not be bossed around and told Destiny that either he must let her be or she could not continue on with him. She knew that if she could not create, she would not exist. Destiny became aware that he could not live without Creation and so he had no choice but to honor her and let her be. Hence their partnership transformed many prospects into certainty. Not long after, Destiny and Creation gave birth to Imagination.

Destiny is a catalyst that pushes our ability to create in response to its circumstances. A situation occurs and we have to do something about it to balance and be at peace with it. We might lose a loved one and have to move, or we might have to find the courage to continue on when we've been knocked down, or we might even have to fall apart before we can pull ourselves together. All the while we are being challenged to understand the question around how important our ability to create is. If our passion is pushing but we are not going anywhere, this could mean we are forcing an outcome. Forced outcomes do not hold sparks. We might eventually arrive at a certain result through this process, but it's not a sparked result because something is missing. It is our trust that allows our most sparked creations to evolve, you cannot push a spark, you have to trust it as if you were an assistant to an artist, and when the artist calls for the color lavender, you go and find it.

Considering that we're in relationship with everything that exists: from people, to animals, to our computer, to our business, to our passion, to our ideas, our dreams, and our spark, these liaisons are quite the affair. Some people are not good in relationships, they can't commit, don't want to be pushed and don't know how to share. In relationship to our spark, we are engaged and about to be married to an energy field that is not in physical form, so consider that our most meaningful stories don't always need to exist in physical form either—at least not in the beginning. In the sense of a real relationship we have expectations but must let the relationship unfold to see if it is a match for us. Our spark is a total match for us; it's our twenty-four carat best friend that will never lie or mislead us, though the caveat is total trust.

A great love story is one that can sweep us into the dance where our partner is the cosmos. In this dance, inspirations flow out from the core of our being and from this state of presence we can stand in any story and spark it. We play the leading roles in our sagas and we have the option to portray our character of choice. We could easily become the homeless person, the billionaire, the psychiatric patient, the terrorist, or Gandhi. Here is my story and of course I made it up, though on many levels I am actually living it . . .

I work for the universe and I am paid in waves of never-ending abundance and bliss. My job changes often, for I am a spark-follower who is on constant call to keep my passion flowing. I have a team of advisors who assist me in all my endeavors. My personal private consultants are consistently whispering soundless wisdom through my intuitive channels, which reverberate into frequencies that tell me where my universal dowry is. I spend lots of time daydreaming, wondering, and focusing on beauty. During the times when I am doing things that are not very fun, I know that I have gotten to an intense part of the lesson and it's time to pay serious attention and not step back from difficulties if I sense there is magic there. When disoriented, I always remember that I am not lost; I am just going in a different direction that I don't yet understand. If my spark dies down, all I care about is getting it to spark again. Are you with me?

This story I invented is my core story. And then there is my realistic story: I am a mother, I have been a salesperson, a hair and makeup artist, a writer, a top-selling real estate broker, a yogi, I love cats, and all animals. I am a great negotiator in business and love the success of a win-win deal. I love Italian food and basically everything Italian, including my Italian husband, whom I have been with for eons. There is also my shadow side story where I delve into my underworld to work things out and do battle with myself; this is where I become humble. Some of those stories go like this: I can't follow rules and I always felt that I never fit in. Sometimes I imagine I was a queen in another lifetime and as a result I sometimes feel a bit entitled and then appalled when I am not treated well. These flipside tales are just more stories that float by, sometimes I invest in them and sometimes I don't.

We decide which stories, we are married to, which stories are unfinished, and which stories we need to divorce from. The energy field of the universe is a conversation; it wants to know what we need, so I am constantly asking for things. I request answers to my questions, experiences that uplift me, and at times I pray to not be swept off by blaring ugliness. I also pray to have an open heart in the midst of darkness and to be balanced and solid when things around me go nuts. My requests to the universe go on, as I am constantly feeling my way to see what will support me. I expect good things to happen that work in my favor, even when they come from bad things that I can't control.

The universe is a delivery service that delivers what we expect. Maybe my high expectations seem crazy but misery seems crazier. I find it disturbing when people are constantly telling me the list of what does not work and I wonder what it is in them that isn't working. Why are they not in the flow of a bigger picture and why are they stuck in the mire of small-minded thinking? Even if something is not working, why are they not creating something else that is? It's the stories we make up that are complicated when we don't believe in magic. Interestingly, we all have thoughts that deliver exactly what we don't want to our doorsteps because our minds went on a holiday to Hell.

Everything going on "Out There" has to do with where our thoughts reside inside. All of our stories carry different levels of density, they hold weight, which creates psychic poundage that's invisible to the eye but becomes apparent in actual reality. You can tell if people cart around overflowing mental garbage by their actions and their energy fields, which are very dark and irritating to others. We must understand that everything we do attracts outcomes that generate either more or less baggage in our lives. Every thought holds energy and we are responsible for our quality of life no matter where we are standing. So if we end up on the sidewalk with a suitcase, we are being challenged to take ourselves higher.

I do an exercise where I gather what does not hold positive weight into a bundle and I hand it back to its source. The businessman who acts rude and inappropriate and then tries to make you think it's your own fault? The nasty cabdriver, the aggressive woman next to you at yoga who has no concept of personal space and keeps putting her smelly foot on your mat, right by your face. All the lovely folks with a nasty chip on their shoulder—hand them back their stuff. Pack the entire dynamic up and energetically hand it over to their higher self in your mind and either finish up what you were originally doing without their stuff or move on. It's amazing that when you hand back other's their stuff, in minutes you will feel a shift inside yourself because you are free of it. Mind you I have picked up my mat and moved spots in the middle of a yoga class. Other times I am stuck and there is no other spot to be in and that is the *"Get Over it Lesson."* I hate this lesson and have tried to hand it to my higher self to get me over it, but they keep handing this one back to me.

We must choose the story we want to live by no matter how hard things are. When things are not right and we can't get over it, the main question is how far astray have we gone? Can we still hear or feel that something is dangerously wrong? We need to realize that because we have been entertaining stories that are not for our highest good that our spark has left the house and we are no longer authentically empowered. These disconnections create fear, because no matter what we do in this state, we are diminished. An unbalanced state attracts an array of low-level mentalities with dysfunctional patterns. We then swirl around in the zone of reactions geared by old wounds and travel farther away from experiencing anything magical or miraculous because we cannot attract that.

One positive thought creates the shift. One scintillating insight brings us back. So while swirling in the darkness, we must reach out for these benchmarks. In order to shift, we must find our light in the darkness and focus on it. As we move into a higher consciousness around any situation, many times the situation has to dissolve or move away, because it has no like-kind consciousness to resonate with. In such a way that we neutralize adversity and decide what to bank on, it's all about what we implant into the matrix of our minds. Correspondingly, invest in visionary thoughts, design your own endearing lifestyle, get into your *joie de vivre*, and use your imagination! Under all circumstances, do make sure that what you think you want is what you really want. Getting a Mercedes is one thing—it's getting to Gandhi that's impressive!

Life is a chorography of movement; we participate by finding our rhythm. We are moving with the tempo that resonates with our pulse. We get into the flow with the cadence of the experiences that move towards us, asking us to partner with them. When the experiences are attractive, we step forward, when they are ugly, we step back. Nevertheless, the great dance might grab us out of our preferences, to swing us around, and unexpectedly set us down in a place where we must deal with worldly events, situations that leave us overcome with anger, sadness, and anxiety. We might be keeled over in grief, but here we are, working it out. It's part of the dance.

Things happen for a reason, our scenarios may shift quickly like a computer springing into the next program; other times while downloading information they run slower than molasses. Sometimes the computer stalls while needing time to adjust, other times it will just crash; we then lose everything and must start over. This usually happens when too much is going on, too many files are open and the circuits jam up. Funny that while editing this book and in fact working on this very paragraph, I was so engaged that I didn't save my work. I went to cut a word and the entire document turned into pages of asterisks. The book was gone. Luckily, I had a saved copy from the day before so I only lost one day's work, but the message was to step away and refresh myself.

We must constantly refresh the connection to our inner spark! Go into the inner desert, forty days would be amazing, but even forty minutes in this modern world will do it. We must train ourselves to slow down and feel the presence of divine goodness. As a child I remember being mesmerized just watching a drop of condensation on a glass expand, break away and release itself down in a stream, I made races out of the drops. As a child I would sing my heart out to no one but myself. When did we lose this sense of wonder? Reclaim it now!

Whatever has caused you to doubt yourself, caused you to believe it's not safe to invest in passions, caused you to think that security is the priority, or that success defines you, please don't believe it! Get out your paints, your telescope, your butterfly net, your fishing rod, your red glitter slippers, and let it rip. Take in all the beauty you can hold, allow yourself to see the enchanted forest through the trees, live out all the clichés. We must let go of our resistance, spit in the wind, step on all the cracks, be old, and wear red lipstick. We must be wild and laugh until we cry, be real, and don't worry about it after. We must be kind to ourselves when our anger is on fire raging, we must be compassionate as our minds are screaming that life is not fair. We must be gentle and at the same time, strong enough to stand in the midst of it all and do what feels right—even when it appears crazy.

When confused, upset, and angry, remember to relax first, and then look at the situation. Relaxing shifts our energy field, slows it down, so we can see what is going on. Imagine a spinning hologram, it's spinning so fast we can't see the image inside it and when it slows down we can see what it's holding. While being able to recognize the truth in a disturbance, we still acknowledge our feelings but they don't over-rule us. Still, in our deliberations we don't need to judge, we just need to get the information we need, use it wisely, and move on. When we slow down, our energy field mimics us and does the same. How crazy is that? Think about it. If the energy field around us is a mimic, then play with it, get funny with it and see if it's funny back. Start profiling passion, goodness, abundance, hilarity, and the accountability of your genius.

In the fleeting instance of a feeling there is more than what meets the eye—this is where magic abounds. Many times your magic is walking behind you, jumping around in your shadow. So play with your shadow, it's what completes you. Sometimes your genius hangs out there along with your inner child who is having a tantrum and they mastermind their way through this warzone together. There is great treasure in the shadow, Friedrich Nietzsche said, *"One must have chaos in oneself in order to give birth to a dancing star."* Carl Jung, the Swiss psychiatrist, wrote, *"Everyone carries a shadow, and the less it is embodied in the individual's conscious life, the blacker and denser it is.*" This concept leads us to be aware of all aspects of ourselves completely. We get in there and come face to face with our anger, our rage, and our pain, as by acknowledging and recognizing our dark side, we are illuminating it with our light side.

We are tracking our treasures through the universe in all aspects of our existence. When passion is on the compass dial, it doesn't matter where we are, all that matters is that our spark exists, that it's activating our curiosity and taking our breath away. As we following this spark, we are shedding an old paradigm—the one that has clouded our view. Our ideas and dreams will most likely be bigger than life, so our world will have to expand to incorporate these castles in the air. As our consciousness expands, it delivers us into new dimensions to continue our creations. Everything that we could ever imagine, fathom, divine, grasp, and dream about, has the potential to exist. Don't let it just sit there, grab it, move with it, take it apart. Let it take you apart. Explode with it like a star. We are stars. We are wild spirits, never to be contained. We came here to detonate our sparks so that parts of us can fly into the wind and change the world. Imagine that!

Reflection:
Envision the light of a star from a far away dimension. Stand in the line of its light and let it shine on you. Ask this light to be your ally, ask it to support you while you are here on Earth, and ask it to empower you to create your destiny.

Now, sit quietly and let this starlight surround you; feel what it does, how it scintillates, how it holds all that there is within it. Explore into it, uncovering all the love you have ever felt, all the excitement, all the dreams, and let it awaken the creativity and the passion that inspires you. Vision the star sparking light like fireworks raining down on you and consider this light as being like a mother who adores you and wants to give you something of herself. She wants you to have some of her light to keep with you. So reach out to this star and let one of her points fall into your hand, hold it gently; tell it that you trust it and that you will always cherish it. Then place it inside your heart and know this spark is with you always. It is your gift; the one you requested and received from the highest source that exists. Every time you lose your way, your footing, your heart's desire, open the release valve to your spark's domain. A spark is full of Shift! It will carry you on its magic carpet and light your way!

The Target
Create Your Reality

Indeed, as I often say, body is the bow, asana is the arrow,
and the soul is the target.
B.K.S Iyengar – *"Light On Life"*

Stories that have soul are alive; they move in patterns collecting their corresponding parts because they are in the process of completing themselves. When a story has spirit, it's bold and goes beyond limits; these kind of stories bypass conventional thought and action. As illustrators of soul sparked stories, we break the rules, challenge the role model, and do not hesitate to be daring. A heartfelt story will not fit in a format; it will be an explosion of passion with a life of its own. This kind of story targets its own reality with the power to manifest itself, it has a destiny—and we are part of it.

An idea grabbed me, woke me up, it made me feel alive. It was saving me, evolving me, making me whole. My idea started to take form; it was becoming real. Others, who claimed to be experts, argued that my idea was not good enough, saying, "I had no platform and it would never work." These experts also said, that I was not doing it well, they said they could fix it and make it work better. I tried it their way, but when I let them in they just kept messing with my magic and ruining my original idea. So I began to protect my now secret notions and hid them away until they were ready to fly. At this point my magical creation then easily came quickly together of its own accord. Finally, it culminated. A large box arrived holding hundreds of copies of the first published book I had written. I had spoken of writing this book for years and teetered with it as a dream, until one day I sat down and began. Its actual arrival was a crowning achievement—just holding the book was enough.

I read this great quote by an unknown author: *"The thing that you do after your day job, in your free time, too early in the morning, too late at night. That thing you read about, write about, think about, in fact fantasize about. That thing you do when you're all alone and there's no one to impress, nothing to prove, no money to be made, simply a passion to pursue. That's it. That's your thing. That's your heart, your guide. That's the thing you must, must do."*

Like the tides affected by the force of the moon, our soul's journey is pulled by the most forceful seduction that exists—our passion. Emily Dickinson quoted, *"The soul selects her own society—then shuts the door."* It is time to open that door, step inside that inner chamber and hang out there until our basket is full. Accordingly, our genius becomes a feeling, which turns into a knowing that we must honor.

Ralph Waldo Emerson wrote, *"The soul answers never by words, but by the thing itself that is inquired after."*

Like the magic in *The Book Of One thousand And One Nights*, Aladdin rubbed the magical lamp to release the genie that granted him never-ending wishes, equivalently; we must stroke the inclination of our genius awake, to fulfill our yearnings. Our genius is the key to our personal specialty that must be distinguished to the highest degree. This virtuosity calls us to step off the line into places that can't be defined; it entices our inventive capacity and sparks our intellectual powers. A great mind will find magic in the ordinary, as great minds travel beyond thinking and reasoning, towards sensing the consciousness in all things. As far out as we go with what sparks our genius is as far out as things are and as far out as things are, is as magical as things become. Our personal originality brings out the essence of our natural attributes and we must employ these attributes because they are our ticket to ride. So if it is our dazzling skill to bake cakes, then this gift will lead to something else, and on it goes until we reach a target. From there we will learn new skills to reach another and another.

In life, our stories are like a movement in dance, we twist, turn, reach up, kneel down, tiptoe and leap, and in the end we surrender all that we have done, and then begin a new dance. The stories we live out are either the tales of how our ego, or our spirit, expresses itself. Imagine honoring who we are in spirit as we are doing the laundry. Hypothesize that our soul-searching is done exactly where we're standing. The spirit of who we think we are is constantly meeting the spirit of who we really are. Once we imbibe the concept that we are on a team with who we are in spirit, everything we do becomes sacred. If you are feeling alone you must imbibe the jazz of your spirit into your step. Our spirit is right here holding our hand, talking to us, walking us through this game of life. One of my teachers had engraved on the wall by her meditation hall, "*Your God Lives In You, As You.*"

Essentially, it is incredible that who we are in spirit is a spark of the God force, we just forgot. We must wake up from the tales we have gone to sleep in and use our creative genius to create new stories—the ones most needed by this world now. When we take the chance and follow our hearts, our stories change. Our true to life visions that are charged with passion, and piloted by the propulsion of our dedicated focus, vibrate, and do not stop until they find their target.

Vibrations always find other harmonic vibrations; they begin to imitate each other. Sound waves resonate with other sound waves and move naturally to the bridge where they commune in harmony to become a symphony. In music the bridge takes one across and at the same time brings us back home to the beginning of the song. The bridge is known as the sequence to transition. In life, inspiration is a bridge, it's a crossover that brings in new ingredients and changes the substructure of a situation. If we don't have inspiration, we are empty, and not the good empty, the yearning empty, then the matter at hand is only about finding what sparks our spirit and lights a fire in our belly. To know what fruit is good in the market we have to touch and smell everything. In life, we can touch it all in our imagination.

In the explorer's mode, we are moving with our spirit. Absolutely, there are times to overstep our own boundaries, to push farther out of our comfort zone, to go for the yoga posture where we may fall over, to spend the extra money, to order the desert, and then recover ourselves. Recovery is when we come back to our completeness. Recovery is not about perfection, it's about honoring the truth, and what completes this truth. Being at one with the source of who we are is to be at home wherever we are. Actually, at our turning points we are the closest to who we are in spirit because nothing else works. If the outer world is an experience of the potential visualized from within, don't get lost out there—get lost inside.

Inside our being is a limitless field of consciousness where our spark exists. The Sanskrit word "*Aditi,*" describes it as the boundless source of all forms. To play with these forms and then step out with them is the new game of pushing our consciousness out beyond boundaries. Another Sanskrit word, "*Dristi,*" is about holding focus on one thing, while at the same time still understanding the existence of all things. It is a gazing technique that in yoga enhances the posture. To gaze is actually to marvel, to seek, to wonder, and to delve beyond where we are. Using dristi as a form of meditation, lets us see the world as it really is and beyond.

How is that possible? We see beyond how we want things to be, to know there is an infinity of other possibilities over and above what we perceive.

Upon meeting the true essence of ourselves, it's as if suddenly everything goes slightly out of focus and another line of vision comes into being. It's more of a feeling than an actual seeing. At the same time we are still seeing, but what we are seeing is the foreground and the background merged, our inner vision is online as if we were looking at duel screens on a laptop. Here we find a multidimensional oneness that draws our gaze towards seeing the perfection in all aspects of what is going on and at the same time our perception asks us to consider what our true intention is, so it may come through. When our mind is focused in a one-pointed way, it stills. A quiet mind is an awesome state that allows for us to recognize that we are being accompanied by who we are in spirit.

Consider taking a dose of an alternative experience as if it were a bridge to be trekked across and we are just going to the other side. Consider going beyond suffering towards a concentrated intention. How is that possible? A flipside mentality is our VIP pass into an alternative experience. Our intention is the actual ticket. Consider going to an amusement park and stepping into the funhouse, we know the floor is not really tilted sideways but nevertheless we are falling sideways and we are laughing. Now create an amusement in your mind, if the tilted floor is a fake, then so may be the amusement. Hang out with your folly and fall sideways with it. Do whatever works and if nothing works, then do nothing. It is rare that we ever do nothing, as we are naturally meddlers. While doing nothing, things are still being done, just not by us. In the same way the soil of the earth nourishes a seed and the sunlight propels it to grow, our energy is working on our visions and juicing them up. While doing nothing our spirit might wander off into wild undomesticated domains to collect things for us. When our spirit returns, together we will make a collage inspired by these newly collected discoveries.

The energy field around a creative discovery or vision moves like wild horses running with the wind. We become great riders of our own inner stallions when we can stay in the saddle and honor the experience. Considering the experiences that throw us off, can we honor something in them that can shift us? Can we go beyond suffering and change the dynamic of who we are around these bronco experiences and ride with that for a reason higher than our suffering? I know a mother that lost a child, the mother in honoring her child's life came to a very powerful place where at the same time that she was grieving deeply, she felt she had to be OK and carry on for her child. She felt as if her child was very close, watching over her. This made her gather her strength to show her child she was all right even though her heart was broken. Her strength gave everyone around her hope that there is a power that can carry us, even when we don't have the strength to carry ourselves.

The art of finding our higher purpose in all dynamics leads us to feel our way around and brings us back to a sparked life. Then again not knowing where our right bearings are is also part of our growth, as we are more open to all the subtleties of finding out. Curiosity, the ability to marvel about what is unusual and extraordinary coerces us to continue on. Our feelings attract desires that amass different energy fields for different reasons, from wanting a pair of new shoes, to packing up and leaving. Wanting the shoes feels like an itch and leaving feels like a big wind is behind us. It's all just energy. The difference between desires fueled by spirit versus those fueled by craving is that the ones fueled by spirit are our destiny. Destiny has a huge energy field that is potent with creation and power. Desires fueled by craving have a low energy field they are needy, always wanting more. Both target satisfaction, though one is transient while the other holds sustenance.

Liberation is the freedom to not be owned by anything, to own everything, to not be restricted, to need nothing, and at the same time to have everything we need. It is a state of mind beyond our normal level of being. The question is can we call forth this state and still stand in a difficult situation? When we can hold a liberated state, we are removing blockages, and dropping baggage, in order to be free, and in this liberated state we can then call forth what we really need to get through it.

Sometimes we have to get off the cultural plane and clear out our low-level mentalities to continue on the elevated track. We've already come to the end of the road of trying to get our needs met just externally, that is the transient way. We must discover that we have the mental power to cope with our pressures and become fearless. A one-pointed inner state is immutable; it clears away debris, it will bypass, throw off, and reject, all that is not important to our greater story. When all that is less than important falls away, it is inevitable that what is pertinent will soon be ringing our doorbell.

Our heart calls the directive and we go with it to get to our destiny. On the way, we must address what arises, this could be a shriek, a broken heart, a malfunction. It's raw and it's real. It could also be a delicate understanding, a touch of love, a release, a new arrival, and a melting into gratitude. As we move through our emotions, we must clear the crazy energy fields, wipe down all our historic cobwebs and come to our sacred haven—a place of emptiness, which holds our palette of creation where we paint our dreams for none other than ourselves.

A state of emptiness is a void that is impregnated with seeds of creation and is open to all possibilities. A void is an energy hatchery that must be programed so its great magical force can come to life. I once had a dream where I arrived into a state of supreme nothing, a dark black empty space. It scared me to my bones and the first thought I had was, "I want to get out of here." Immediately, I woke up. All day, I could not stop thinking about this weird dream and started researching voids, since I had no idea what they were or how to use them. I discovered from my research that a void needs a thought form to progress. If I had requested to feel love and bliss, then I imagine I could have ended up seeing Heaven. Voids are portals into a great energy field, so if you place a seed in a void it explodes to life. Imagine sitting in meditation and opening a void, throwing your magical seeds in there and then letting the energy of the void do what it needs to do with your seeds of creation.

Imagine creating a void in the midst of a calamity. Sitting down to meditate in the middle of a huge disturbance might seem insane, but to be free from mental disturbance is sound sense. The more empty space that exists within us leaves more room for us to breathe in new life force. What goes on around us does not have to affect what goes on within us. So when stuck in a circumstance that is painful try opening a void and asking for some fuel to strengthen your heart, ask for some enthusiasm to alleviate your depression, ask for some joy.

Our target is actually the point of convergence where our enthusiasm meets reality. Once we define it, our vision will have fuel and start to move. Then the energy field of creation does what needs to be done to make things happen. In Shavasana, the yoga posture for relaxation, we have to let go of everything to get the benefit of this state. My yoga teacher, Rodney Yee, describes this pose as the most difficult posture in yoga. A friend described one of her Shavasana experiences as not going to sleep, but going into a state where crazy mind and all the dramatic happenings going on, dissolved. She then had a great revelation about her life and what to do next.

Anchored into relaxation, after our menu for what we will eat today, and what we will do next, calms down, then as our mental texting fades, an enlightened vision may pay a visit. As we vision, we touch upon every ingredient and play with thought forms that are impregnated with charged ideas that have the elastic potential to rotate around what exists, and still hold its ingredients. Can we do the same? A potent idea will test us to see if we are strong enough to carry it. The idea, in order to manifest, needs us to stay with it. Even when we are tumbled with a wave of dissolution, we are just being made stronger to be able to carry the idea as it grows. Then the idea becomes solid filled with its own kinetic energy and off it goes.

Inside we all have a warrior spirit, who like the chariot driver, controls the reins of all that affects us. In Hinduism, the word *Abhyasa* is described as the determined effort of the disciplined mind. Empowered with *Abhyasa*, we control where our smaller mind goes in order to allow our higher mind to take the reins. Just in the thought around our higher purpose, as we look at our beliefs and actions to see if they match up high enough, things fall away. Giving up the sinking ship describes the Sanskrit word *Vairagya*, the practice of letting go. These two sacred companion practices of *Abhyasa* and *Vairagya* support us in mastering our minds while letting go of what is not good enough so we are able to sit on the peaceful throne as the higher being of our true self.

Some of us will do great things in the world, but a higher purpose does not demand that. It demands we do great things within ourselves, things we feel good about, things that sit well with us. We did not come here with an assignment; we came here to be great beings for ourselves alone—this in itself is our offering. Personally, I am in pursuit of equanimity, a state of steadiness laced with tranquility. It is one thing to hold this state in a daydream, or a yoga class, and another to hold it out in the world. Even when we lose ourselves, this state exists, and to step into it liberates us from our hell. It's a practice to maintain this credo that offers us a level of comfort that can't be had from any other source. Here, we no longer need to question our abilities, meet our match, or be good enough for others, as there is nothing lacking, no deficiency. We are just in the process of understanding the greatness of who we really are, synonymously through our mistakes and our moments of hopelessness, because our turning points keep delivering us home to ourselves.

On my first day of first grade, I had an experience with an abusive teacher. She asked the class a question, I raised my hand and said the wrong answer, and then she then called me "Stupid." In that moment the world stopped for me. There was a decision to be made. If I had believed her words, they could have caused me great suffering and possibly long-term damage, but they didn't. This teacher did me a big favor that day, as she was the catalyst that pushed me into no longer believing in any program other than my own. Connected into such a high state of wonder, I refused to give it up, shut it down, or homogenize it. So when my teacher called me stupid, it didn't affect me because I was so securely stationed into myself that she seemed insane to me. I felt so much pleasure in my inner life that I was satiated. Granted, I was six years old at the time, but it really doesn't matter at what age we acknowledge this treasury.

In the moments when we are being challenged, the outside world, our wrong thinking, or a flash of fear, might momentarily define us, though nevertheless, when we feel discomfort it's our spirit calling us home to our real world. On a path that targets the shape shifting of our reality we must not believe or invest in stories that don't support or invest in us. Our words and underlying beliefs create our reality, therefore everything single thing we mentally invest in counts.

After achieving major success in the real estate industry, a new agent approached me for help. She wanted to know if I could share my tricks and was curious as to why my success looked so easy. I explained to her that my passion was what motivated me and described how I'd imagined and visioned this fortunate outcome. I described, how once I had this clear picture in my mind, I simply hooked into how good it felt. In wanting to own these feelings, I anchored into them because I knew they would lead me right to my outcomes.

"It happens the way I believe it could happen."

"No! That is totally impossible. It can't be true," she responded.

"That is the truth," I said.

"How can you just assume that you'll always achieve a certain outcome?" she asked.

It was a difficult concept for her to grasp and it made her mad. I explained that I had desired and believed so much in my outcomes that I felt they were bound to happen. I pointed out that my choices for this particular profession at this time were not haphazard. I had a goal and it was not just about money, it was about the experience being rewarding. I needed to feel victorious around these concepts to see if they were important for my life. In the beginning, being successful made me feel exuberant, but then I lost my passion. It ran off because my ego was doing the money dance. I then learned that a true sense of success had nothing to do with money, only passion. Funny that when I realized this, my passion came back and was stronger than ever. It was because I had defined what was important to me, and passion rules. I cannot be on a journey that is not impassioned; I would rather just sit and read books, my other passion, until my passion comes back.

Our explorations may be a wild ride of accelerations and cessations, a mix of launches and landings. We will fly, and we will crash, but after awhile our crashes are not a big deal. The up and down action becomes like a sun salutation where we stretch to the sky to salute the sun, and in the next moment, we are on our knees and our bellies kissing the ground. There is wealth in all our postures, so when we land face first smack on the ground, we are being asked to change perspective. The message is to no longer be controlled by what appears to be or what we believe is circumstantially possible. In a child's world everything is possible. When we cut ourselves off from our source, our targets become obscured, and we live in reaction to feelings we can't handle. We do things for all the wrong reasons, like to cover up shame, so we fill up our canvas with things that have no passion, and then we feel the wrong kind of empty, the painful kind.

My friend's father was the town drunk. After school, his mother would send him to retrieve his inebriated dad, who was usually out cold, snoring on the sidewalk. My friend's shame was so extreme that it impelled him to become successful at any cost. Sadly his success never fulfilled him because his motivation did not stem from a place of personal power; it was a cover up. Meanwhile, storm patterns kept developing for the purpose of sabotaging his efforts to continue this ruse. It was nature's way of trying to take the covers off so he could experience success for his own reasons.

Our historic conditioning is just another exercise plan that calls for us to work our stuff out, to muscle up and change who we are in response to what was established. What is most noteworthy is who we are now and how memorable we can make this significant experience. When painful feelings arise that need dealing with it's time to make sense of them, time to take in their meaning, shift what needs to be revised, and release the bad feelings so that they can't hold us hostage. Speaking of histrionics, a close friend told me her mother called her after a day they had spent together to ask if my friend still loved her as much now, as she did when she was little. This pushed a button that made my friend feel like nothing she ever did was good enough. In thinking about this I wondered what exactly was triggered inside my friend that made her feel that she was not good enough?

It's interesting that the deep-seated feelings we harbor are usually reflected right back to us in our relationships and experiences. When we feel we don't deserve things, they don't come to us. When we feel we are not good enough we are treated as such. Therefore, when things come up that are disheartening there is an opportunity to find the matching dynamic in ourselves and address it. My friend and I played with words and came up with this response: "Mother, what part of you does not know how much I adore you?" In fact, this is the exact dialogue my friend must have with herself. Imagine looking in a mirror and asking yourself, "What part of you does not know how adored you are?"

We no longer have to hold our historic hot potatoes that game is over. The new game is about cutting the cords on these old rooted situations that hold us back. This could mean searching inside ourselves for where the old cords are attached, and cutting them from there. Sometimes we must first do mental calisthenics and scrutinize our personal collective experience to see what has transpired from what is at hand. When we magnify our unconscious mind, we then expose the things that are not good enough to support where we want to go. We address, disbelieve, and clear our past impressions, so that we can look fixedly into a future we want.

When I started my career in real estate, I worked in a very competitive office where a new broker was not welcome. A couple of my co-workers, out to sabotage me, ransacked my desk, kept disconnecting my computer, and made up lies about me to get me to leave. I guess they were threatened and believed there was not enough pie to go around. It quickly turned into a mean, angry, aggressive dynamic. There was literal acrimony in that office, I knew it was a tough business, but this was insane.

I was curious as to how and why I manifested this situation and was geared to hold my own beyond all that goes on in a crazy atmosphere. Repeatedly, the relationships we have out in the world are reflections of the relationship we have with ourselves. Our negative thought patterns are the gatekeepers of the stories that hold us back. These stories are wake-up calls and the goal is to get to the bottom of where they come from, how they manifest, and project something else to change the scene.

Regarding my real estate comrades, I considered leaving, but felt I was abandoning myself by giving up. It was time to look deeper into myself while experimenting with different thoughts and feelings about my officemates. Firstly, I imagined them in a van careening off a cliff and realized this would not change the dynamic. I then questioned where I was sabotaging myself and what beliefs I had that could have brought this situation on. I saw flashes of my long-time notion that I did not fit in. Bingo! I had always held up this idea like I was proud of it. But when I really looked at it, it seemed that the underlying message in it, was that I should be gotten rid of. As I continued to go deeper into this belief, I realized I was the one who did not want to fit in. I had rejected others, judging them as not good enough and used the "not fitting in" concept as an excuse. No wonder this dynamic was attracting meanness and hostility—I was acting condescending.

I immediately decided that I fit in perfectly well and made the choice to manifest peace by changing my historic patterns. I refused to hook into my officemates shenanigans; instead I continually held out a peace offering. The situation transformed quickly as one by one they apologized. To shift it, I had to own my part in the situation, which brought into focus a truth I needed to see in myself and understand how it manifested itself in the exterior world. This is scary stuff; to be slapped in the face with our unconscious shenanigans come to life. In the bigger picture we live in a crazy time, so to constantly delve inside and take apart what does not uphold our decorum is all we can do. I am constantly writing a news flash about myself, here's one: "She held her own beyond all that goes on in a crazy world!"

Sometimes things are called treasures because we have to find them. It's about seeing what is special in a situation that needs to be unearthed. If you can't find your treasure, take everything apart, sort it out, keep looking for something satisfying, and if it still does not exist, then make it up. The ticket is to own what we are creating even when it has not transpired yet. In a manifesting mode we must liberate our beliefs, as in confidence with ourselves, we are being asked to believe in something that is non-existent though in the process of coming to be. We must trust that we are partners with the magic of the universe and everything that happens is part of the plan. We must protect our great expectations even as we're bombarded with opinions and judgments. And we must stay in a state of continual creativity even if we are just lighting a candle and blessing an idea.

While writing this book, I hired an editor who was trying to make my words sound, as she said, "Normal", my resistance brought out her edginess. Actually, she was better at putting me down than editing my work. We must impose limits on the time spent falling prey to these things. It's like a war maneuver, we go in fast, free the inner-child hostage, and get out. At the end of the day with this editor, I learned a few things about writing that were helpful, but I mostly learned not to hand my creativity over to someone who is not on my frequency. This was a great lesson and worth the expensive experience.

The potent heart is a truth slayer that always knows the pertinent questions about a person, place, or situation. The answers are instantaneous. The mind complicates things; it opens all the drawers and messes up the mentality of the room, while the heart is like the trial attorney that has no further questions. The heart knows instantly if something can be used for the good and where the treasure is. The heart knows if love exists, or is possible, because it is just recognizing itself.

We might feel lost at times, but when we are in balance we are lost in the perfect direction. Being in balance is a more subtle movement than stillness. In every action, thought, and stance, there is always a counter position, balance is found in-between them and touches upon both positions. Consider hitting a target, the balance is found between aiming and firing. It's a moment of total trust where everything is centered.

Every little thing that happens has some sort of symmetry around it and when you look at things from a wider perspective they will actually tell you what they need in order to be in balance. Therefore, to hit a most honorable target we must transform hate into love, discomfort into acceptance, and difficulty into success. We must do the opposite of what our small-minded egos are clamoring for. So when slapped, we do not automatically slap back. Instead we hold still and we choose to participate only in the actions that are motivated by our masterful ways. Great battles and treasures are won this way.

A Japanese warrior, whose motive was to taunt his opponent, bragged loudly, "I am a better warrior than you, as I have the power to pull out my sword and chop off your head for no reason." His opponent smiled, whispering, "And I have the ability to let you do just that!" This powerful statement instantly seared the braggart-warrior's heart. He then got down on his knees and asked to be accepted as student of this holy teacher who in one breath transformed the egotistic stupidity that was coming at him.

Mastery is a solitary journey where we are on our own with all aspects of ourselves. There is no school for this course. It is simply between who we are in spirit and who we are in human form. We are our own teachers and we define our curriculum to find our work of genius. Whatever action is called for, when empowered by our purest self, it travels through all dimensions and pierces all realities, never stopping until it reaches its target. The target comes into focus; the bull's-eye is hit and has no choice but to manifest.

Hitting our target is the metaphysical mind-play of quantum physics. It's about our interactions with the energy fields and how we affect them. We imagine, we create, and we charge up our creations with love. You don't have to physically show up, there are no real bows or arrows, and there is no real target, and no real bull's-eye. It is the partnering of our mental capacity with our heart that decides the next destination.

We set one's sights on the landing place, hold a one pointed focus, ignite our passion, and then we hit SEND!

Reflection:

Unlock the trunk that holds your longings, recover all that you fancy, take your dreams down from the attic, blow the dust off their wrappings and wander aimlessly within their utopia. Forget about what's valid, we're cruising in unbound space, so let go of gravity and weave into where your passion exists.

An idea will come, let it unfold, travel with it. This idea needs you to be its sun and culminate its seeds. Your creative energy field is its soil and your genius is the farmer. Now, step into the story you have surmised, find where the joy is hidden and let it unfold. Imagine this creation as a baby bird you are throwing up into the air to fly. Imagine it being held by a magical universal energy field that is going around and collecting all the ingredients needed to manifest your imagined design in the way that is best. Imagine this bird of creation that you threw into the air as a homing bird on a mission—your mission. This homing bird is collecting your goods and will always find you wherever you are. Then again, it has a secret to tell you and the secret is: A little homing bird will always find you because you are home wherever you are. You are the target and this bird is the free essence of you that is delivering you back your dream.

A Leap Of Faith
Affirmations of the Soul

"Belief consists in accepting the affirmations of the soul; unbelief, is denying them." -Ralph Waldo Emerson

One morning I noticed a squirrel scurry up to the highest limb of a tree, pause, and then fling itself into the air. The squirrel's arms and legs were outstretched like an airplane's wings—it was flying. Time stood still for me, until the squirrel landed on the next tree and ran off. I knew that feeling of the squirrel believing in every cell of its being that it would make it to the next tree. This reflection reminded me that in our leaps of faith, we are being held closer than ever by a great supporting power.

Imagine gliding on magnificent wings, feeling the release of everything that weighs you down. It's time to let go and soar. Crazy mind inevitably comes online to drag you back to your old way of thinking, but spirit tells you that you are now stepping into a bigger vision and you no longer need what you had. Our old patterns will not work at this turning point because we have a clean slate. We are immersed in a sacred transformation where we get to unravel and shred until our new wings are formed.

Radical change demands that we stand on an entirely different foundation than the one we stood on before. We have arrived at the bridge, an elevated place, a crossover between two points or ways of being. We arrive at this new place with nothing but who we are. After all, we are going to paradise, and everything we need, will be there, so we let go.

In order to arrive in paradise, we must question the concepts we've lived with all our lives, we must soften our fixed ideas of what is right or wrong, and focus on leaping out of bounds. Most of us have been raised to believe that we need security in order to feel good. We are geared to fight to maintain the status quo. It's ultimately a cruel joke that we have been trained to rely so strongly on the material world. The truth is there is no real security on this earthly plane; our only real support is on the spiritual plane. So we can spend our days building nests and collecting nuts until the moon turns to cheese, but until we look inside and discover our real treasure, we will never be secure.

True security is an agreement we make with ourselves, when we know that we are okay no matter what. When we operate this way, as our higher selves, we don't need a safety measure because we are one. Real security is inherent in higher states so we no longer need to look for it anywhere else. Imagine being excused from doing the tick-tock dance, or having to sing for our supper, or having to do anything for any reasons other than a feeling of innate rightness.

Granted, we will still have to do difficult things, but we just blow through them because we have a date with our bliss and can't hang out in drama.

Living in a higher state is a practice. Much like in yoga class, we warm up, and then we move into the deeper more potent postures. By warming up we are preparing to surrender our habit of holding back, and at the same time, we are not forcing anything. In the act of surrendering we are vulnerable, a condition most humans abhor and go to great lengths to avoid. As we spend time in the struggle, we wonder why sometimes we are not moving forward and the reason is because we are fighting the flow. Nothing is moving against us, we are moving against it. The key to living in a higher state is knowing when to step forward to assist and when to stand back, in order to let the energy do what it needs to do. Sometimes we must allow ourselves a time out in the midst of a challenge, a moment to catch our breath and acknowledge the sweetness that exists. As children, it was so natural to lay in the grass and watch the clouds pass, though as adults we need to travel back and find the mindset of our youth to rediscover that joy of playing and dreaming just for the sake of it.

Children know how to maintain their dream worlds, which are so valuable to them. So let's sit around and make up some stories: "I'm on my own private jet on my way to Italy for dinner with friends. The next day I'm shopping for a villa to spend weekends in springtime there." What I'm manifesting here is not necessarily the jet, the villa, or the friends; it's simply a feeling of happiness that I experienced in a daydream. My cells don't know the difference; they just want more of this feeling of joy. Allowing my daydreams to travel, I take my hand off the wheel and let my dreams drive. They bring me to amazing places, places way beyond what I personally perceive is plausible. Then again in what is considered the real world, maybe my bank account is low, my friends are all busy and I am sitting around like a goon daydreaming, but it's no surprise to me if I end up at an Italian restaurant in Brooklyn, where over dinner, I'm invited to Rome.

The god force shows up in the weirdest places. My husband, who is also in love with his espresso machine, was in the hardware store reading instructions on a coffee-machine cleaner and thinking about how totally toxic the ingredients were. Out of nowhere a fellow passed by him and said, "Use baking soda, it's not toxic." When we're in the magic zone everything is connected, the flow is open, and everyone is on our team. Ever have these days? They are mysterious and marvelous. Other times we are so busy in our heads that we miss the messages. We wander around looking for them and in fact, we wouldn't notice one if it fell on our head because we are not in the right zone to get the magical memorandum.

This kind of disconnected state delivers us to the "Time Out Zone," as our unconscious activities can only go on for so long until the consequences kick in. Time outs are necessary shelters where behind the scenes our magnificence is still there actively directing our next storyline. We think we are on hold, but we are being held, for being withdrawn from our game is part of the plan. Like an arrow, we are pulled back in order to release farther. So our retreats are potent manifesting times, dreaming and traveling times, for we cannot launch without time spent in this sacred haven. These retreats are not punishments, we are still in sacred space, and nothing has changed except our timing. In the future when it appears nothing is happening, consider that your spiritual alliance might have gone off to the gas station to get extra fuel because they knew you would be flying farther than expected.

I was put in time out often when I was a child and I always used that sacred time to fly away from all the silly things expected of me. In the domain of my imagination, I let go of what I believed possible and let my inner child put in her requests. She naturally always asked for directions on how to get to the party! And of course, we are always on the guest list, as it's our party. On these excursions, I was out there in an expansive state of mind, no longer stuck in the limited concept of *"Just Me."* A friend called it "Shifting from ego to we go." Where are we going? We're going to visit who we are in paradise, the relaxed blissed out versions of ourselves. We are playing around in another dimension where end results don't matter—all that matters is that we are now in our own blissful actuality. When our now is full of pleasure, we are abundantly suffused, and there is a sense of rightness about everything. Every time we take this trip into to our all-inclusive utopia, we trigger our real sustenance. Maybe we can't live on daydreams, but our daydreams magnetize to us what our soul needs—and our souls then manifests what is viable. Maybe in our everyday reality, nothing is moving, and we feel stuck. At these points, we need to ask ourselves if what we are expecting is aligned with who we are in spirit. Are we moving with our essence or our ego? What aspect of us is driving? When things are not moving, we are being called to focus, and not on where we're going but on how we are doing.

A friend recently told me her five-year plan for becoming a successful artist. Her storyline felt exhausting. I told her to forget the plan and just get lost in the bliss of making her art. She thought about this for a minute and then thanked me as she knew she needed the experience of feeling the pleasure of the end result now, to create it as viable. The success story and the art story are two different stories. I have felt successful finishing something very personal that no one would ever know about. On the other hand, I have felt empty standing on a stage receiving awards for business achievements when my heart was no longer in it. To me success is personal, as when something only has external significance, it just feels like work, but a significant internal triumph is a breakthrough. The former originates from the heart of who we are and the latter stems from the idea of who we think we need to be.

When we take a break from making plans and just live in the moment, we create room for serendipitous experiences to arrive. Just arriving into the now with no expectations, being open to what comes as if on an adventure is enough. Even when nothing makes sense, things can still feel right. We are being asked to go beyond the realms of reason, to bypass what is logical and allow our magical fate to whisk us away. The greatest turn arounds happen at the oddest times because in unexpected moments we drop barriers. As a child, "Go to your room," was my greatest gift in the form of a punishment. I would lie around dreaming, singing, and talking to my invisible friends. ·

A friend told me that, one day, while strolling in Central Park, she saw a very handsome man petting a dog and in that very moment she felt a stirring in her ovaries. Paternity at first sight targeted her and there was no explanation. She knew right then and there that she would be having a child with this unknown handsome dog-petter. Not long after, she married him and had a son. She told me she had no desire to have a child prior to that day, but the moment she set eyes on her husband to be, she clearly heard a message inside saying, "This man is the father of your child."

When we hear potent messages that are abstract, it's time to pay attention. These strong statements are coming from higher planes. Yes, they are weird, but weird is our new homeland. And yes, it's greatly weird that we would be in conversation with voices from beyond. How great to tap into the unearthly zone and go out-there where our stories can suddenly flip on dime, and where new situations arrive in the strangest packages. Weird is good, it's just not normal. Mystery is the wonderful adventure minus the plans. Remember, as children the pleasure in a mere treasure hunt, a game of hide-and-seek? We need to go back there!

Maybe this entire chapter is another daydream in written form, then again what is more genuine, the harshness of reality, the struggle of existence, or the boundlessness of an adventure? These are all just stories; our hearts decide which ones pull us in. Some people do not need to enter other worlds, the magnificence and magic in this world is grand enough to deliver them into a state of awe. This state is a gift. A simple blade of grass can seem like another world when you place it under a microscope to see its cells grow and watch its chloroform move. All that is exquisite, including the moon and the stars, exist within us. Is that possible? Our minds have the Magnifying Glass App. We can expand on anything, so why not use this great App to expand out into an awesome state of being? Try it for a day, just for the fun of it.

My yoga teacher Rodney Yee, who sometimes reminds me of the perspicacious Yoda from *Star Wars*, is always saying wise things in between postures. One morning he said, "Focus on an object so deeply that you become the object." It takes faith to even consider an experience like this, because we have to let go of who we think we are to truly understand something else. We have to move beyond restriction, what is impractical, and go beyond the impossible to merge into something else.

Belief Banking is a partnership we form with our G.O.D force aka Goodness-On-Demand. This is the currency that procures our supreme interest, which also has a return rate of endless possibilities. How interesting that all the money that passes through our hands in America bears the words, "In God We Trust." All day long, people pass around the written message to trust God, and yet, they're not really aware of what they're doing. We hoard these green pieces of paper, trading them for the material things we need, when all along it's only been our beliefs that have allowed us to have or not have the things we want. Imagine how you would feel if you understood that God bought you a cup of coffee! Everything we have comes from our Universal Banking Account. Our account balance depends on our ability to flow and knowing that the password is: *Gratitude*.

Most successful people are risk-takers who learn more from the ventures that don't work, than from the ones that do. We always have to go beyond our limitations to understand we have none. This life is all-inclusive, so order the works. There is no reason to limit anything when there are no limitations on miracles. My friend Agnes was sadly selling her family heirlooms. I asked her why she was letting go of her dearest possessions and she replied that she had no money.

"Never say that again," I demanded.

"Never say what again?" Agnes asked.

"That you have no money," I replied.

"What do I say?" she asked.

We were now playing with words.

"I _____ money. Please fill in the blank, I requested."

"I *have* money?" she asked.

"Repeat it," I said, and continued to push her to repeat it until she said it with conviction. I watched her mind stop as her mouth was stating words that her consciousness deemed impossible. She looked into my eyes, and I read her mind, which was deciding, using logic, whether it was possible to have money when she didn't know where it would come from. I asked her why she cared where it came from or how it arrived, as wouldn't its arrival be enough? Her mind stopped as her consciousness began to shift, she was detaching from her dogma.

What if one day you got a strong urge to change your entire life? What if you felt a yen to reconstruct everything you have built, a desire to shift around all the little pieces you've created for security? Your inner voices are telling you to *"Sell everything and Go,"* as some strange undefined courage appears out of nowhere to assist you. We've all heard stories of how a distant friend just picked up and off they went. We might have thought they'd gone crazy but behind that thought, our spirit cheered their spirit on.

I met a fellow on a jungle beach in Costa Rica, floating in a tide pool. He had been a very successful hedge-fund manager at one point in his life. He told me he had *"completed his marriage,"* and explained that seeing it this way had left him great friends with his ex-wife. In the interim, he left his job as a banker, moved to Nosara, and was teaching

6 a.m. yoga to surfers. He was beaming with happiness. He had rescued a big, floppy dog that was his new best friend and he realized he did not need much to exist and be happy. He was living his dream.

What if we no longer should-ed ourselves, and just followed our spark? What if we no longer listed and judged all our difficulties? What if we just let go of all that? I doubt we'd arrive in Hell. It's more like we'd be stepping away from there. Imagine enjoying life for its adventure and playing it out like a fun game. We don't need to walk on eggshells or play it cool when we are busy taking a chance on our wheel of fortune. Suppose that none of what happens is real anyway. What if you were told by an impeccable source that this life is just like a dream and just like in a dream, the suffering is temporary? What if you knew that you could wake up any time? Would you ever hold back again?

Consider tossing all misery to the wind. Take yourself out on a date, pull the *"Take a chance"* card and drop your baggage. We don't know the outcome. We don't know what blessings will come to be, but in our bones we feel blessed. This reliance on faith is based upon embracing a light-hearted attitude, our *Que Sera, what ever will be.* The mindset and energy of this perspective is not solid like a rock but under its surface, it's more stable than a mountain.

At a turning point in my life when I was not turning with it, I had the excruciating experience of greedy people in my business trying to dislodge me. At the time, I was in a strong partnership with what I like to call "my inner witch doctor," so information and guidance started to come to me quite quickly. A friend emailed me an adaptation of "The Paradoxical Commandments," by Dr. Kent M. Keith. The lines that spoke to me were, *"People are often unreasonable, irrational and self-centered. Forgive them anyway . . . In the final analysis, it is between you and God. It was never between you and them anyway."* This took me deep down into myself to see where I needed to strengthen my relationship to the divine. After sitting and meditating, I opened a book by Deepak Chopra to a line that said, *"Every decision I make is a choice between a grievance and a miracle. I let go of grievances and choose miracles."* I knew that I had to invest in the faith of these teachings, and that if I did, they would transform me. If I obsessed about *what was on my plate*, along with *who did what*, and *how dare they*, I would lose all my goodness, my life force, and my success. So I chose to bank on the teachings that would elevate me above people's malice.

In the everyday world meanness, ugliness, cheating, and cruelty abound, but we can gently remove the hooks, clean the wounds and reinforce our goal of not having to be immersed in pain. We must reach for an invisible hand to hold, while we walk across the rocky paths. When we are going beyond our best options are usually not the obvious ones. There is always another scene behind the scene and sometimes we must wait for the fog of emotion to clear before we can see at all. When things are not clear, it's best to do nothing but play with mental possibilities. When one starts flashing, we are onto something. Confronted with other people's disharmony, if there is nothing for us to learn from it, we easily move on, though if there is something in it to grow from, we must roll up our sleeves.

I met a customer while selling real estate, who the minute she set eyes on me, the chemistry went to Hell. She was rude, condescending, and her behavior was nasty and out of control. I was polite but gave the keys to my partner to lock up and quickly left. Driving off, I thought I had gotten away unscathed but realized this nasty woman had bothered me. I wanted to find the power place to not be affected by these kinds of difficult interactions with nasty people and I got my chance as the woman requested another appointment. That very morning, my teacher Rodney mentioned the practice of *tonglen* in yoga class. Tonglen is a Tibetan meditation practice of breathing in difficulties and suffering, and breathing out love and happiness. Ding! Here was my solution. I was committed to succeeding at this practice no matter what the woman did or said. Interesting, that when the rude woman showed up, she was as nice as could be. In pondering this, I realized I was so committed to the *tonglen* practice that the energy had automatically shifted. I did not have to do the actual practice in reality because I'd already done it in my mind. When we do whatever it takes for a breakthrough, the miracles are already aligning to create the desired outcome.

If we consider that our difficulties are an opportunity for growth then we must be on the lookout for where our potential breakthroughs exist. Many times they may be hiding in the heart of our most disturbing situations. In a one-pointed evolved state of mind, we bypass the dreck of the disturbance and go right to the source of its prescribed wisdom. The goal is to move through our discomforts on the way to our party. It can feel like taking a twelve-hour flight to paradise: the flight is uncomfortable but the moment we feel the warmth of the sun and hear the birds singing, we forget the discomfort. So when Ms. Pain knocks, open the door, give her a good meal, a bath, and put her to bed. She didn't come to torture us, though sometimes it feels that way. She just wants us to take care of her and calm her down—with love. At times when Ms. Pain is ignored, she rises up to become the uncomfortable catalyst that propels us forward. We must remember that this discomfort is only temporary; she is just trying to get our attention so we can transform what is needed.

Faith is a decision, a resolution, and a commitment that becomes the bridge from one realm to another. It's like stepping into an elevator and pressing the evolution button to arrive at a higher mental level. The door opens and we step out into a radical breakthrough. On the advanced elevation there are many expansive options when we choose things that move at a higher frequency. The advancing momentum of an energy field of faith looks like sound waves; being in its flow, is being able to surf all kinds of waves including waves of discomfort. Life and energy fields have many currents, and comparable to the ocean there are sharks, dangerous rip tides, sweet dolphins, and starfish in the waves. So every time you are confronted with what is hideous in life, remember that amidst the ugly there is also beauty and sustenance. Faith asks us to hold on when we are trying to survive; to hold on when things go out of control and nothing makes sense, because the universe has a plan that we are part of.

My friend, an alternative healer in Texas, was having incredible results healing cancer patients with oxygen therapy. The government warned him to stop his practice, as he was not licensed or FDA-approved. He ignored them and was sent to prison. Stuck there for two years, he could not understand why it was in his destiny to be locked away from doing such good. One day there was a prison riot and a fellow-inmate's main artery was slashed. My friend saved his life. When the ruckus calmed down, he heard a loud and clear voice inside say, *"This is why you were here—to help this man."* He was mysteriously released a few days later and then moved to Mexico to continue his healing practices.

We don't always know upfront, why, or how we end up where we do. We can analyze what we did to get there till the cows come home and still not have an answer. If where you are is not where you'd like to be, try to enjoy it anyway. Pretend it's not permanent—because it's not. It is our responsibility to change the paradigm of our state of mind. Sometimes it's as simple as simulating a good mood in the midst of Hell, other times it's about finding our strength. We are being taught through our constant challenges that we can handle more than we thought. I read somewhere that when we are thrown to the ground; our soul is in our knees. When life gets heavy I look to my heroes and imagine what they'd do. I always hear Martin Luther King, Jr.'s booming voice declaring, *"I have a dream,"* and his last lines, *"Free at last."* Hearing this excites me, and reminds me of my passion. I realize I left it somewhere and need to get back to it.

The art of freedom involves grabbing our own bliss. We must show up for ourselves knowing we have the power to transform anything. We can slip through the cracks and call our minds into free-play if need be. And we can be so darn grateful for every little thing, including the things that don't work out, because we live in the total trust zone. Imagine being okay in the midst of conflict, as fluctuations no longer affect us. We don't have to run away from our experiences because we can shift who we are in them. Our freedom lives in letting go and realizing we've released the arrow and it's time to let it sail towards its target.

Rodney Yee spoke one morning in yoga class about the difference between focus and force. He described how focus aligns the posture, while force can push us out of alignment. Miracles reside in the quiet moments of allowing; we are focused, our intention is on our target and we are letting it come to be. As Belief Bankers, we wait with faith, knowing that our inner confidence comes with a heavenly warranty. The seeds of our magic are planted. We don't have to worry, the weather is perfect, and our sustenance is growing. We have already done what was needed—we planted the seeds. Like a chef preparing soup, we gathered the ingredients, threw them into the pot, and lit the fire. We lovingly stirred and waited for the soup to cook. But who actually cooks the soup? There comes a point when the soup just cooks itself, it just does what it's supposed to do. The farmers after planting seeds do not sit out in the field watching the corn grow; after they've plowed and tilled the fields, they go fishing and the corn will just do what it does.

Certainty is aligned with the word *amen*. Amen is usually said at the end of a prayer, and means *"So be it."* It is also used after a statement of truth to express approval and support. How interesting that *abracadabra* basically means the same thing: *to create as you speak.* To honor the magic of the spoken word is to give kudos to miracles and grace. Consider the word *hallelujah,* an exclamation of joy, praise, and gratitude; just saying it can enhance its meaning. These words access a state of being where we may relax and rest assured, because what needs to be is as it should be, and what is meant to arrive is on its way.

Open your front door, the one to your heart, and offer your bliss as currency. Call out your version of *"Amen"*, holler and shout *"Hallelujah"*, worship your dreams and sing praise on your heart's way. *Abracadabra!* We are doing it, leaping off the edge to fly, this is the turn around—so be it!

71

Reflection:

We are going on a joy ride. Let your heart have its way. Let things fall apart when they are wavering. We no longer have to hold everything in place. Why be held in place when freedom is an option? There are possibilities for freedom in every point of view we encounter—find them!

Create your own beliefs, honor and fortify your exemption from misery. Our state of mind is the ticket to our authority. Toss everything that holds you back to the wind. Throw negativity into the sun to burn away. Clear your energy field and invest whole-heartedly in your passion, your joy, what rocks your world. We are at the plateau where we can live in our truth and it's paradise here. Our commitment to living this way transpires naturally when we simply can't stand to live any other way. There's total relief in living like this, because we are no longer stuck, wrong, bad, or otherwise. Antoine de Saint-Exupery, the author of *The Little Prince,* wrote, *"I know but one freedom and that is the freedom of the mind."* We are just in the process of moving through it all and feeling our bliss while doing it. Abracadabra that! Amen!

"The amen of nature is always a flower."
– Oliver Wendell Holmes

Fear-Less-Ness
The Hero's Journey

"Let everything happen to you
Beauty and terror
Just keep going
No feeling is final."
–Rainer Maria Rilke

"Good gracious! Holy shit! Damn!" The exclamation and excited utterance of emphatic verbal release is the cry out loud when we are thrown through a loop. We have all experienced a close call, a narrow escape, a heart stopper, and a brush with our death—many times. The suspense we feel as we white knuckle our way though terror, leads us to find out that we were running on the fast track to our own heroism. Imagine standing on the other side of fear, knowing it was the catalysis to your freedom? To be able to acknowledge a darkness that exists, but to remain unaffected by the action of it, is to disempower it. It is the reaction that enhances all actions. In a tough situation, to hold ones own, precipitates the fact that we have become the agent of change we are looking for.

The challenge is to release ourselves from the culprit; a low-level perception of sneaky dark speculation with octopus arms that will devour our hope. When the trick of craziness is up at bat, we must bat away lunacy. I went to a real estate course on ethics and compliance issues, the entire course was about what you cannot say and do—ever. To be successful in business you have to know the rules, to be successful in life these same ethics and compliance rules apply to the mind. As in "No, you may not think that, no you may not act on that thought; we are now being quiet and doing nothing." Sometimes we must wait and make no decisions until after the fire dies down. The best way to enter a burning house is by knowing if we should just let it burn to the ground and walk away—even when we have to start again.

We are all energy readers, we have the ability to interpret what appears to be and feel the energy of all things. In order to bypass mental gibberish, go by your gut, the Japanese refer to this area as the Hara, a potent energy center that is tapped into our Chi, which is our life force. The hara is a portal or a gateway, which we can pull in or expel energy out from. The solar plexus is a wisdom center that is way more knowledgeable than the brain; it goes by instinctive feel and incorporates all the senses to act as an antenna. When one senses emotional pain, it hits in the gut. The gut is an open sensory radar station that comprehends information and has the ability to digest the life force that nourishes us. As a physical organ, the stomach has its own brainpower in the sense of knowing what is no good, what we don't need, and quickly sending it to the colon to be gotten rid of.

Fear hits the gut first and then spreads throughout the entire body, even into the hair follicles. It coagulates, builds up mass, gets blown out of proportion and surrounds us to take us down. This trepidation might slam in like an earthquake disrupting everything around us, or like the jitters, it may sneak upon us in the middle of the night, wake us up, and shake us to the bones. Fear's goal is to radically stimulate our impulses to trigger the pathfinder within us. Being that we are pioneers on the soul frontier, sometimes we are like squatters, other times trailblazers. Either way, when fear shows up we must own the fact that it will affect us, and cause us to do something about it. On the ethereal plane of mastery, it always strikes a note for us to remember that we are a palpable presence with the ability to disburse fear's energy.

We've all had those *"up at 4am and walking around the house"* kind of nights. On one such particular night, after an intense dream, I was wide-awake before dawn when magic happens, having the why conversation with myself. I brewed some tea and then checked my email to find the word of the day from Dictionary.com was "Kobold", a bedeviled spirit, gnome, or goblin. The kobolds haunted dark, solitary places and were often seen in the mines. The miners named them kobolds, after the word "cobalt", a toxic metal that forms ore deep in the earth. Cobalt is poisonous, containing arsenic that was known to kill miners. Interesting that I would learn this word on a morning my mind was filled with trickster thoughts. I reckoned that those tricky kobolds have moved out of the mines, and into our minds, where they sit cackling in our dark corners, creating doubts, and trying to make us ill.

Upon further investigation on the period from which the word "kobold" evolved, I read about a haunted house in England that sat empty on the market for years. Men who considered buying the house spent evenings in the living room armed with guns against a ghost, but fled when the apparition actually showed up. Finally, a courageous fellow arrived unarmed and waited for the spirit to appear. The spirit showed up just after midnight, rattling chains. The prospective buyer followed it into the dining room, where it vanished. The next morning the man had the floorboards dug up in the exact spot where the ghost had disappeared. There, they found a decayed corpse buried in chains. The courageous buyer had the body exhumed and properly buried in the cemetery down the road. He then proceeded to buy the house for an excellent price.

Fear is a call for healing, a challenge to wake up, toughen up, and do something about it. On the other hand there are times it seems fear is valid; it has reasoning and is a warning that demands attention. This leads us to wonder when to consider if something is real or not. There is a slogan that states, *fear is false evidence appearing real*. Consider now that real evidence may not be real either. What we consider *real* is inasmuch about our perception in the moment. What is real in one environment does not hold true in another environment. It's all a matter of how we look at it, for instance the bed is real, it's solid, and exists, but when we go to sleep the bed is gone.

Energy is alive, even though it's invisible; it is felt and does things. Many times fear is misunderstood because it's really negativity, a mass of displaced energy that tries to attach to people, places, and things. Negativity is a vampire-like dynamic on a mission to suck the life force out of all it comes in contact with. We all know some vampire-like people that we feel drained by, and after ten minutes of conversing with them, we are exhausted. A masterful psyche fields the layers of negativity that bombard us, even when our own mind creates vampire-like thoughts that tell us lies and drain our energy. Negativity is just displaced energy that is not helpful and a good trick to dislodge it is to replace it by doing something else. Rodney Yee while teaching a beginner yoga class said, "It is the everyday ritual that pierces darkness." This is why I go to yoga, to pierce my darkness. Other than that I clean my house when I need to discharge negative energy, my house is very clean. Going into nature reminds us of the beauty this world holds and that we must hold it too. We must do whatever it takes to dislodge and transform darkness, walk around the block five times, sing, take a bath, sit with animals, hug a tree, do something, anything, to shift an overcast field of dark energy.

In the modern world of computer technology and the information highway of supposed real time, our psyches are constantly being bombarded with too many stories that are steadily playing inside and out. It sometimes feels like we are walking through the television section of a shopping mall, where multiple screens are blaring all around us. The energy patterns out there are as variable as the weather causing extreme pressure with a high craziness index. We suddenly get into moods where we have quick tempers and falling-outs, because we are unprotected in an overcharged information field. Most of this kind of information is just static that exists right outside our front door. Holding a consciously high state is our protection and keeps the good energy around us no matter where we are. It's a vicious cycle, to get lost on the mental dumbed-down unconscious treadmill of the daily grind.

As a consequence, it's time to get off, and mostly on ourselves! We do this by changing our programed channel and reducing the volume of loud background interference to tune into, and turn up, what we love. It's a challenge to hold our eloquence intact, which as such, reflects the strength of our convictions.

One morning, I took a video of my yoga teacher in deep meditation before class started as about fifty people were speaking extremely loudly, all around him. He was gone into his own state. When we are immersed in our own state, we are busy doing what gets us off this constant battleground with life. Being in touch with what moves us and what sets us free, puts us right into a high frequency zone, and so as the exterior annoying or challenging stories bump into our stories, we have a baseline and a foundation that we come home to. We don't have control over the state of the world or other people's behaviors, as all we can affect is the quality of life in our own little realms. So we hone up to clearing congestion, swatting away lunacy, and holding our own. Mind you my Yoga teacher said he likes to meditate in crowds because he loves the workout.

A friend with a young daughter that I had not spoken to in a while, told me at fifty, she was now getting divorced and changing her career as a commercial artist since the world is no longer supporting her business model.

She said "It is not easy for people my age to start again and be successful."

"Will you be OK?" I asked

"Of course!" She exclaimed boldly.

She then went on to define who she was in a very heroic tone. I realized about the vibrational power of our stories. This example of two stories bumping into each other, one being that the world was not supporting my friend's career and it was hard, and the second story, which my friend admonished: that she is a survivor. This second story had much more power, so it would override the first story. It would have been easy for my friend to have empowered the first story more, but she chose not to. This got me to thinking about how we use our stories as excuses for why it is the way it is. Why we have this addiction, this disorder, this malfunction, and why it is not our fault.

Really? You think a story is set in stone, what about when something else suddenly happens, Prince Charming arrives, our pumpkin turns into a hybrid jeep, the wicked witch dies, we are free. Granted we all have valid reasons to become addicted to pain medication, we all have pain, but, the stories are not set in stone, it is our mind that believes in them and cements the stones across the door to our chamber. One by one remove the stones, acknowledge each stone in itself is not that heavy and can be lifted. Have a conversation with the stones, *"Hello mother, it's not your fault I never felt good enough."* Smash! Each stone is a little story we are taking down. If the wall is years long, then like Milarepa, the most widely known Tibetan Saint who after an evil act became enlightened from building and taking down a tower over and over; we too must do whatever it takes.

Holding our own is key, because we don't need to hold anything else. Holding our own is changing our dialogue and our movements so they collaborate with the state we are empowering. Equivalently, this state is the same state that empowers us. Even in the process of our death, we have control over the quality of our moments. The late great, musician Lou Reed was doing *Tai Chi* with his hands as he left this world.

Holding our own calls us to make conscious important life-changing choices, including the ones that may cause discomfort, like a break up, a job change, moving, forgiving, or following our heart's desire when the odds are against us. If things are not working and we sincerely did all we could, we must do something radical. It's a radical move to follow our convictions and to build our foundation on them. Radical moves begin with radical beliefs, mine are: I don't need to abide by society's standards, or buy into a group mentality that is based on values I don't believe in, even if they're accepted by the masses. I will not measure my beauty or financial status against *normal*, and I don't need to invest in tired stories, as I am exempt from them. I am a work in progress and nothing I do is final. Are you with me?

We must defy what we don't believe in, in order to breakthrough what holds us back. It takes moxie to not agree with the status quo and rev up the nerve to do something else. So we go out on a limb, if it breaks and we fall on our ass, we dust ourselves off and keep going because we have a purpose that is beyond an end result. Sometimes, we are called forth to sift through a pile of dung, hold a stiff upper lip, be gutsy, and do what it takes. Maybe we become the crazy mother who fights for her child against a bad school system. Maybe we become the spy who tells the world a big secret. Maybe we are the ones who protest, who pray, and who care deeply as our calling. We are busy changing the world around us. Even changing the world just in our house, in our job, or in our minds, makes a huge difference.

We have to leap off the edge to care. A great writer is not afraid to crack, as a hero is not afraid to bleed. A great chef is not afraid to be burned, and a boxer expects to be hit in the face once in a while. It's part of the paradigm, as suffering is part of a life experience. As a child I hated sleepovers and I always wanted to go home. The other child would always come up with an adventure to get me to stay. It's the same with being in this world; there are times we want to go home, as everything going on is all too much. We get overwhelmed and can't be part of the adventure because there are too many crazy stones piled up.

Robin Williams, the actor, a man with an immense spark, made us laugh for so many years. He took the dark and ugly; turned it inside out and exposed it. We all agreed there were demons, he showed us how to play with them, make fun of them, exposed their bullshit. Every time one man goes down, we all go down. We all share the same pain and the same joys; we all battle our demons and teeter on the edge at times, so we can't judge another's struggle. It is a private affair when such a good man with such a potent spark decides he cannot take his pain anymore and takes his life. We have to come to terms with the fact that even our heroes have pain. We live in intense times, it is often a horribly harsh reality, bad things happen, craziness; depression is a monster sometimes—we all fight it. We understand the pain, the fear, and the heartbreak, because we all share it. We must have great compassion for a fellow being who in his way changed the world for the better— many times. When he fell overboard, our hearts went with him because he left behind a legacy of his love and his struggle.

We came here to be heroes who follow our truth, and many times that is not an easy journey. Ask yourself do I have the strength to roll up my sleeves and keep going? Can we show up for ourselves when no one or nothing else does? Can we take the expedition beyond the mind into the heart where we can project our hope, our positive ideas, and enlightened prayers? If we can compassionately understand inner dynamics that need help, we can show up for ourselves even when nothing else does.

Our painful emotions either strengthen our ability to gain a clear perspective, or they push us to grow from them. Coming from the zone of the heart, we process things differently, honestly, and nobly, because hearts are majestic and can impress upon all that confronts them. Our being is vibrational—we attract what we need. Our minds need so much, while our souls only need to continue the love. Can we hold love more than angst? Granted there are times angst is valid, but many times it is just a habitual pattern. We must replace the patterns that don't support our truth with what does, even when we have to make something up. If we define angst as a lie, which it is, we then get to decide which lie we would rather believe.

Every emotion is a vibration, if we don't play with pulling up the vibrations we want, our emotions will decide for us. They love the roller coaster ride, the house of fear; they don't need much sleep, as they love making havoc in the night. What part of us is ready to jump into the dark waters at a moments notice? Let's name this entity "Ms. Plasma." Her scenario is that every time Ms. Plasma walks down the street and sees something disturbing, she runs right over to get involved, picking up on all the particles of panic and pain. She then gets on her cell phone and spreads the panic and pain to all her buddies so they are now infected too. She uses the news on television to overstimulate herself every night before bed, and when she wakes up after a few good nightmares she's ready for a whole new day of mental infestations. She's totally controlled by fear, but doesn't know it. By the time the latest crazy disease actually arrives in her town, she's so stressed out, that her immune system is shot and she has a bull's-eye on her back, flashing "HIT ME!"

We are constantly confronted by warnings that are terrifying: an economic crisis is coming, nuclear war, bio-terrorism, hurricanes, tornados, pollution, genetically engineered food, bad water, oil spills, nuclear leaks, chemical warfare, animal torture, Ebola, more wars, and conspiracy theories. This litany of terror is a bombardment of darkness. It's not kid's stuff; it's real and happening. This kind of terror is emotionally paralyzing. It has a lack of morality that stresses us out, makes us furious, and horrifies us; and these are the vibrations that run through our nervous systems to make us feel reactionary and desperate. Manipulated by high states of fear, we enter the red zone. We might feel hopeless that we can't fix it, but we can oppose it by continuing to hold our good state. In the meantime we do what we can.

Remembering the times in my life where I had been robbed of things, the feeling of unfairness, the swindle of being ripped off, and the anger at the disrespect. I would quickly replace the things taken with something else. There comes a time when we have to empower ourselves even when we are emotionally robbed. If all my hope is stolen and I am in a puddle on the floor, then how I grab it back is to not succumb to believing the communal lie that not having what I need is normal. Our planet is overrun with material things that have nothing to do with gratitude, but much to do with the word "More!" All the subliminal messages out there brainwash us into believing that we do not already have everything we need and we need more to be okay.

How about buying into the fact that we have exactly what we need? How about doing the opposite of what your ego wants, what the world wants, and rather than rushing to accomplish something, try standing still first. Get in touch with what you really have and if it's nothing right now, then the message is, "You are going on from here because you are still something."

It does not matter one iota *where* we stand, but on a heroes journey, it matters greatly *how* we stand. Being aware that we are standing on a living growing powerfully divine planet, feeds us energetically. Put your bare feet on the earth, be aware of the earth's magnetic healing frequency, pull it up and in, and nourish yourself with this earthly energy field—it's called grounding. We must honor the warm up to our great acts. In yoga, before we go into deeper postures we stretch, we don't just go right into handstand, we warm up to it. In life we also have to stretch ourselves out and release the resistance before a good move. The warm up is as important as any action because we are honoring where we are and building up our leverage before we leap.

My favorite yoga pose is *Tadasana, mountain pose,* a simple standing pose, legs grounded, spine erect, shoulders open, head balanced over the heart, arms alongside the body. Seems simple, but this is a powerful pose that harmonizes the body and mind, increases awareness, develops strength and flexibility, expels depression, increases energy, and boosts enthusiasm. These are just the mental benefits. You don't have to be a yogi to do this pose; it can be done anywhere, the supermarket line is perfect. It's a two-minute life shift, a reset into balance that alters our mind.

We wonder, is it really possible to change an energy field, define a new direction, blow through a maelstrom of fear? We can! We shift it by building up our positive frequency, tuning into harmony, and carefully integrating the harmonic aspects of we want into our reality. We play with ideas and forms, and build structures from them. Every time I think of something going on as bad, like so-and-so did something awful, I make up a new story, a little vignette, because I don't want the bad story in my energy field. Maybe my new story will never happen; nonetheless, I have a good energy field.

Define what makes you happy, get on the carousel and grab for the ring, the one where you marry yourself because you have fallen in-love. It is not easy to live like this, to sift through all that does not work, to go for our heart's calling and live for love. Immersed in passion, we have an intestinal fortitude of resoluteness; it comes with endurance and staying power. Furthermore, no matter how good we are at creating our residence in Pollyanna-Ville other dynamics happen, events transpire, and we are challenged to do what needs to be done. Consider the case of finding ourselves lost at a crossroads, caught in distress, feeling the first waves of depression, and believing we are in a swell of irreversible momentum—we've all been there. These are events that illustrate an emergency advisory message to forewarn us that it's time to shift once again. We are receiving a wake-up call to reroute us out of a mundane existence and root us back into our source. This red flag asks us to identify everything in our life that is not moving us towards our highest self. How amazing that the universe is literally requesting us to validate our pass into what we believe in. We are being solicited to define what is more important, what we dream, or what exists.

The question is can we use a disturbance to our best advantage, maybe related to the sense of setting ourselves free? After a deep and intense yoga class, my teacher Rodney Yee said, "The irritations we feel are where we are burning in purification." This led me to understand that I should no longer take my irritations seriously. Every time they come up, I now think, "Aha—purification." Another time he said, "The grief that you have in this moment is where you are working." So what we're dealing with is either the pure grief, the fear that there will be more grief, or the fear that we can't handle the grief. Just in this one thought, that we can't handle what's going on, we undermine ourselves. When we enter a panic zone, we are being called to face a fear with the opportunity to gather ourselves. It's time to come to light with what to move on from, to consider these hazardous times as openings into a new portal where we can be heroes, this might be fancy thinking but taking stock in a thought is like investing in futures.

An enlightened story is one that imparts knowledge and essentially builds a new foundation, which can hold us up. Like magicians we have to transform the ugliness, the pain and the greed, by being otherwise. Granted, every day we are called to act as scouts who go out to the frontlines and report back to ourselves. We all witness the disadvantaged, the wretchedness, and everyday and we have to transform it. To alleviate and alter all this we have to digest the chaos, pray on it and offer our heart to it, knowing that because we care we are piercing it with love.

Concocting new ways to dispel darkness and bring in more light is a potent antidote. There is always something helpful to do, feed people, give things away, hold the door, don't react. When I go to yoga, I arrive early to set up the mat for the teacher; sometimes I sweep the floor, other times I set up mats and props for strangers. I don't work there, I perform selfless service there and it feels like a gift for me to offer my support. I love doing it. It also stops me from sitting there and blabbing before class. I hold these classes as sacred and so they deliver sacredness to me. We must understand that to regard our activities with reverence can make a simple activity worthy of being divine.

In staying out of the line of fire, we must track the eye of the storm and not stand in it so it will have less power over us. Consequently when trauma kidnaps our inner child and runs off to hide in the woods, we must become like a shaman and simply go out to retrieve ourselves. Instinctively we are hunters and what more importantly is there to track down than our real selves? In our pursuit of happiness, of magic, and wisdom, it is through the integration of all aspects of ourselves that we can reclaim these things. As we bring ourselves home we have the ability to rehabilitate what is broken and bring it back to life.

Our minds try to make sense out of things when really it is our senses that know how to maneuver. Introspection will help us determine whether our difficult emotions are valid or a ghost from the past. When a difficult emotion is valid, it's giving us an important message by telling us it's time to change. When it's a ghost from the past, it's a bunch of old patterns that stimulate tired stories, trying to revive them. Our ghosts from the past just want to remind us of our previous pain by constantly bringing it back to the surface, only so that we might heal it. When we heal it, these ghosts don't exist anymore.

Fear resides in voices that hold us back. *"Watch out or you'll be hurt,"* they call out. These fearful voices live like viruses in our nervous system and flare up at a moment's notice. Inflamed, they spread negative thinking, disbelief in ourselves, and paranoia to take us down. Paranoia is a viral pattern that can quickly infect one's psyche. It opens the door for those tricky kobolds that hover about staging all the what-if scenarios. Paranoia's best friend is neurosis, defined in the dictionary as hysteria of the nervous system. Neurosis is a syndrome that distorts our balance and coerces us into reacting from the dark places inside. It mimics, magnifies, pantomimes, and stages craziness. Paranoia and neurosis feed off shadows creating phobias that shut us down. I Googled phobias and there were hundreds: fear of dust, wind, sitting down, thunder, water, and other people. These phobias seem very real but like kobolds they are just controlling little monsters that need to be brought to light.

If we operate out of a fear-based consciousness, we are possessed and the way we behave is reactive and defensive. So when fear, paranoia, and neurosis, surround us like a force field, the first thing we must do is sit quietly and disconnect from it. These emotions have cords that tie us up and we must mentally cut them. At the same time we must continuously pull our energy away from the black holes, step over the cracks, change the channels, and replace the locks. We lock out guilt trips, threats of love withdrawn, relationships based on games, bad moods, head games, power trips, and all that does not support us. We break the subliminal contracts we've made that keep things distorted. Likewise, pertaining to relationships, we usually expect others to be who we think they are, which leads us to never really accept others as they genuinely are. Then, it's as if the relationships we're having are not actually with other people but only with different layers of ourselves. The other people are doing the same and we wonder why we're lonely. We need to be clear with ourselves, pure with our intentions and upfront with our hearts to set people free to be who they are, not who we need them to be.

A young friend told me she was living her life to keep her parents happy. That she no longer had any idea of who she was and what inspired her. She was angry and was shutting herself down with drugs, nicotine, and bad food. On top of all this, she told constant lies to keep her parents comfortable. This made her feel bad about herself; she was running on the hamster wheel. If we no longer made crazy subliminal contracts with ourselves, or agreed to protect old family wounds, or acted against our best interests to maintain someone else's comfort level, then who would we be? We would be free to find out.

Thoughts are currents and we tend to ride them, especially when they are strong. We can get lost for long periods in a thought moving downstream. At this point the dynamic becomes not about moving forward, but about coming back. Being lost is a refusal to deal with what is here. Really, there is no such thing as being lost; it is just about the acceptance of where we are. We spend a lot of time arguing with ourselves, talking ourselves into things, as opposed to really listening and seeing what is going on. Our inner child has needs, our ego must have that dress, our passion needs perfume, and since we're tired it's okay if we sleep late. It's time to go to the source and listen to our higher self, to sit and delve beyond all our neediness, and travel into a place of freedom. Here, we wander around in our own wilderness and we find that what we really need is what moves us in spirit.

I read a quote that said, "Fall seven times, stand up eight." My yoga teachers always encourage us to fall over in class. They love when students move beyond the posture to a place of instability. Balance is just a continual act of losing and finding symmetry. It is the same with our pain and emotions, we must learn how to sway with them, and breathe them out, so that they don't become solidified in our psyches. So consider that when things are not going well, possibly we are practicing the art of falling and coming back. In truth, we are being asked to be OK with imbalance because on the edge, falling is mandatory and so is leaping.

I was sitting in my office at work late one gloomy February afternoon, thinking about why I lived in such a cold dark climate where night begins to descend so early in winter. Looking out the window at the bare trees, and the dirty gray snow, I was feeling depleted, and missing the warmth and light of summer. Depression was hovering. Suddenly a van pulled into the parking lot and out came a band of holy Buddhist monks in bright orange and yellow robes. They were going next door to Starbucks for tea, so I followed them just to be in their presence. Approaching their interpreter, I asked if they would come back to my office and offer a blessing. The head monk who spoke no English, nodded yes. The monks arrived moments later to loudly chant their mantras. It was such a sincere blessing. After the monks left, I thought about how the light always arrives in the darkness, and how sacred it was for the universe to send me a band of monks to make me smile.

Everything that is happening around us is a great opportunity. When we see it this way, we can transcend anything!

Reflection:

Sit still and prepare to swab the decks of all your negative mental thoughts, intentions, and ideas. Pull up your story of the month and get ready to edit. I'm sure you have at least a few; you can do more than one. Write it out, listing everything that bothers you in the story, everything that does not work, everything that is upsetting, and edit from there. Start cutting out all the parts that are not good enough and add new parts, just re-write the story. Don't worry about what warrants reality, just consider the reality you want and re-write from there. Rewrite your story the way you need it to be. Rewrite it to put you in your power. Rewrite it in a way for you to feel good, for things to flow. Don't judge anything you are doing here, just do it—write, and if you can't write dream. When you are done review the new story, this is your cutting edge story of the month. No matter what goes on out in the world, honor and uphold your story, keep remembering it, vision it. This charges it up and magnetizes something potentially uplifting to arrive because you have changed your energy field.

To hold our own: we get rid of all that does not support us in spirit and collect everything we want that will. We bundle all the goodness we can muster up and carry it with us like a talisman. This abracadabra protects us; it dissuades away darkness, holds light on our dreams, and keeps us on our hero's journey. So step forward with discipline and honor, armed not in defense, but with pure intentions. It was intent that pulled the sword from the stone. The sword is our power and the stone is our fear. Grasp your sword and pull it out of negativity and own your power. When you grasp your power, the stone will let go because negativity has no real hold.

Transformation
Our Evolution

The only way to make sense out of change is to plunge into it, move with it, and join the dance. –Alan Watts

You can't hold on to a pole, a rock, or a hard place, when the winds come, you will be swept away. When your heart opens you will be swept away. When sadness arises, you will be swept away. When you let yourself dance with abandon, you will be swept away. We came here to be swept away by the winds of life, so we must become light like feathers to lift off and flow.

Tabula rasa, a Latin word that means "blank slate," and signifies the primal beginning of the beginning—before anything. The first letter written, the first stroke of the paintbrush, the first idea, the first sight of love, the inception of knowing, a sacred inspiration, are all the starting points of creation. In holding our consciousness clear of experience and perception, we will nurture ourselves by our divine inspirations. Inspiration is described in the scriptures as something being breathed into by God. Another poignant definition of inspiration, interestingly, is the natural process of inhaling, as we are breathing our spirit back into ourselves. Take a deep breath of energy, spirit essence, and magic; and inhale the scent of creative arousal. This is the essence of what is grand and sparks new beginnings, be it an unmerited gift, an expression of love, beauty, a breakthrough. A clean slate, gives us the ability to constantly refresh our inspirations, for as each one comes to be, there is room for another.

Innovation is our drawing card, a mental refresh tab where we keep things interesting and alive. The same old one hit wonder will always hold its great essence, but after a while we cannot travel on it. The reasoning aspect of our consciousness is always on the line to define what is, but it is our super-consciousness that knows when we must switch over to a fresh operating mode. In the manner of physics we can change one form into another form of energy, we can transpose what is ugly into beauty by recognizing beauty. There is still beauty in agony, in transition, and in the sincerity of spirit, no matter what is going on. Sometimes beauty stands in the background enticing us to look beyond while she is doing her calisthenics. She is strengthening herself for her debut where she will come out in all her glory and grab us. It is the moment where things appear to be one thing and out of nowhere there is an awakening midst of something else. All we are asking of ourselves is to see what is on the upper shelf, and to drag a stool over to reach it.

To believe in goodness and beauty, even in the midst of darkness, keeps what is light-filled alive, and even when we don't believe, we are still held by this goodness. I held hands with my mother as she passed on. I witnessed her gasping for life and saw her fear. I saw remorse in her eyes for what she thought she did that was not good enough and how she disguised those things. I witnessed her final surrender and knew that when she could not reach for a sense of divine beauty, it finally reached for her and enveloped her. I knew, because I saw the smile on her face as she left this world.

Our sparks of insight are significant events that are personal and inspire us to make life-changing decisions. For instance, we decided to get on the plane, we knew it was over and walked away, we chose the red dress, we cut our hair off, we said yes. Such unquestionable decisions have a mind of their own because they come through a charged divine force field where the directives are beyond doubt. These kinds of notions are so affirmative that there is no need to mess with them. Such indisputable insight leaves an impression that moves our emotional DNA around—it literally shifts us.

In the meanwhile we still have to drive and when the direction becomes confusing, in order to know which choice to make, we mentally play with the outcomes: the beginning, the ending, the arrival, the departure, and all that goes on in the middle of the stories we are collaborating with. If we feel pulled by an aggressive emotion, it's best to do nothing. If the picture is not clear and we don't feel pulled in any direction, it's best to do nothing. Doing nothing is like stepping into a force field for a download of fuel. This vacant zone is a region that might seem empty but actually encompasses everything. To travel into this void is to let go of what we are holding onto and reach beyond for our magical goodness.

A magical sparked consciousness always exists around the parameter of who we are, but sometimes like a dog it runs off into the woods to catch the scent of a new inspiration. Sometimes it goes so far that our state of mind needs a moment to catch up and then we must go after it to retrieve this new incentive of our genius. This action of bringing ourselves back to the table is all that needs to be done—over and over. We go out, we explore, expand our horizons, and come home, to rest up to do it again. There are no meaningless moments. Everything counts. Even the weird feelings that push us count, as they are pushing to get past them. We have taken off the training wheels so when we slip off the curb into ancient emotions, we must realize this is old stuff and not who we are now. This way we are not attracting the same old thing but different new things. And as we walk into the unknown our rational mind will try to talk us out of it, anxiety tells us we can't rely on the unknown, while fear whispers, *"You're taking a risk? Forget it."* Hopelessness tells us that we are not good enough and it will never work out. Finally, our inner authenticity declares, "This is the only way I can actually live!" And in this powerful moment everything else quiets down.

The only relationship that is accountable is the one between our heart and our spirit. Granted, there are instances where we are not going to be comfortable, we get an itch we can't reach, we're stuck between a rock and hard place, we've tripped over our own feet once again, and we can't access our spark. What the Hell is going on? We are being pushed to work with this grand dose of "Ick," until we bypass all the mental schisms that block the door to our promised land. Our testimonial stamp of approval on just being OK as we are is the first key in the code to enter our promised land. That is enough. We don't have to complete anything, as just holding this personal testimony is enough. Martin Luther King Jr. did not personally have to go to his Promised Land; it was enough that he paved the way for us to get there, and left the gift of his promise for the world to stand in. He already lived in his promised land and his life was his offering.

We too, are living in our promised land. This is it. We have arrived. There is no end result, no prize to achieve; our peaceful holy state of mind is the prize. So what do we do in this great state? We wash the dishes, we take the dog for a walk, we show up to work, to class, but the difference is, that *we really show up* and dance our ass off to our own music. We are still standing where we were but just in a higher state—with a shift of consciousness.

Imagine if your higher mind ran off and took your illusions and woe with them and dumped them in a garbage bin, then you would have a moment of what it's like to be free. This is how we need to live, to be free to breathe our inspirations, and to possess love for who we are and what we do. Our quality of life is a decision we must buttress. Eventually as our state becomes solid, we live completely in the now and nothing has to uphold anything because everything is just part of the experience of living in a holy state.

Our highest self does not thrive on outcomes, it thrives on the experience. Only humans are geared to live for end results, and once we reach them, there is the next one, and the next one—we are not satiated this way. To really experience great wisdom and mystery is to stay in the moment. Everyday we wake up and we are not the same, only the stories we hold onto remain the same, and every morning we try to fit ourselves back into these old stories as if they were our shoes. We are growing out of our shoes and our stories are falling apart in the exact way they are meant to, so we can be part of new ones!

Our emotions blare, when we no longer want what we had and our pleasure has run off and left us dry. We can't go backwards to a comfort zone that no longer exists. At this time we are nowhere, and this feels crazy as we are being called to reckon with the reason for our existence. We didn't come here to be comfortable, we came to connect with our passion and offer it out. It's time to stop and take a moment, an hour, a day, a week or even a year to justify what state we are committed to thriving from. It's a great moment when we interrupt all our patterns, push off the edge and wade out into the unknown. Unfamiliar experiences have the power to awaken us. We cannot be bored in them because we don't know the workings. To find oneself in an unfamiliar experience is a gift to expand with. We must pay attention here because there is something to learn; we can't do things in the same old way, and we've already mastered the old game so there is no further reason to play it. To continue winning a tired game is to stay stuck. We are going beyond where things are far-reaching and all embracing. We are going way past the familiar into a new version of possibility.

Crazy mind is not the culprit but the advocate for stepping away from zombie consciousness. Being normal is a fugitive boring cognitive process of reasoning, with conclusions that compartmentalize things. If you look out there at what is considered normal (aka captive), you will see through the fabrication of lies, to know that normal is the height of insanity. There is nothing-normal going on; it's just a program. To fathom what is beyond knowing and reasoning is to go into the dark with a flashlight and root around where nothing makes sense. How can we use our mind to our advantage without being tethered? We either become like the rock set hard in the river knowing what we know, or the moving river itself that explores the world. We rotate around these dichotomies when it is time to be still and time to flow. Really the only reasoning that is viable is the reasoning that sets us free.

A state of mind is usually referred to as a temporary state. This reference works when we are acting crazy, having mood swings, feeling depressed, and so on. We can then blame it on our temporary state. To untether the mind from old patterns we must use the mind as a resource to not get caught in the trap of normal thinking. The normal mind with all its rules is so tired it can no longer stand up because being average is exhausting. What wakes us up is the fact that we have roughly a hundred billion neurons in our brains all synapsing, deciphering, and sending out orders. Our neural pathways are waiting for our exciting new directives. It has been proven scientifically that when new ideas are imposed upon mind neurons, the ideas are grabbed and assimilated. We are on an epic adventure that like an action movie includes the horror stories, the love stories, and our story. We decide which story we are investing in.

The choreography of our stories are in constant motion, people come and go, we age, we leave, and we come back with a new story. Our evolution is never static, even in moments of stillness there is activity going on. In meditation, our bodies are breathing, pulsing, digesting, our brain waves cross synapses, our psyche is awake, our souls are traveling, and we are dreaming while manifesting our futures. It might look like we're just sitting still, but inside we may be moving mountains. Imagine taking a big chunk of what is not working along with all the emotions around it, imagine calling a moving company, loading up all the emotions and sending them off to the ethers. Just doing it in our mind is enough. So inflect on a space where your spirit can dance, roam around the house, the world, and find new inspirations to be part of. Hello? Mentally we are moving mountains here, the ones we created. Though, in physical form we are just sitting there meditating, watching our breath, or looking at the colors behind our eyelids, and meanwhile our imagination is out there performing for our benefit.

In alternative realities, we clear the cache of all that is patterned to keep us the same, mainly the habitual conformity of our thoughts. Granted, our raw feelings might be the moment's reality but they are not solid or everlasting. How great that these dissolutions flash across our screens to be dealt with so we know exactly what needs to be replaced. I always get messages on my laptop that new uploads are available, do I prefer to upload now, later, or tomorrow? This is the question; do we want to deal with change now?

As we slide along the edge, we don't have to do it right, it's not the time to edit creations, or arrange things so the outcomes are acceptable for others—great art does not come from that. We just have to keep sliding, as we might have to blow through an encyclopedia of beliefs to get where we're going. When we play with reality, there is no short end of the stick, it's still a stick, but we can make it a wand, a fishing pole, or a whip—we decide. The edge is just the end of one way of being and the beginning of another. To slide on it is to journey out to meet ourselves and create our future from there. I heard a statement that not doing the right thing is expensive, then again, anything other than doing the right thing is either a great lesson, or worthless. In the middle of instructing a warrior pose, my yoga teacher Rodney said, "Things that have less integrity blend in with everything else." This thought exploded a recognition of that's why it's important to keep things high—so they don't enmesh but become sacred.

While holding our integrity, we write, paint, create, dance, dream, do amazing business, even just do the laundry, but the difference is we are holding an evolved state. And if we are in the process of falling apart, to do it with integrity allows the space for us to come back together with new parts. Creative liberation with integrity is a state of being entirely whole and undiminished no matter what. We ignite who we are in spirit to illuminate the space around us. Spirits are free to fly and many times they are just feeling their way. Right now, there's no time to waste clinging to what you think you know; it's time to feel your way. We are being called to wake up because our good energy is needed here—right now. A quantum alteration is converging. It's time to switch tactics, to yo-yo and flip-flop out of automatic, and into manual. It is our destiny to unravel, unroll, untwist, and untangle ourselves from our cocoons to feel how to fly

Reflection:
We're off to see the wizard, the wonderful wizard of Us! On this Yellow Brick Road we are now taking an about-face and walking home, now. Forget about begging a fake wizard for information, forget wearing anyone else's shoes, forget

about the good witch too, we're done with these games, even if we have to live in a world with a bunch of munchkins and we still have needy friends who are always on a quest to find what they already have. The Wicked Witch is now our best friend, and most importantly, we are the real wizards! So be that, it's who you really are.

We are the perfect combination of all aspects that exist and we are going to divine our way through a new paradigm where we prevail perfectly well wherever we are. Pack your bag and put your empty basket outside the door with a note that says, "Ready for an adventure." Lift off to be carried by the wind of change. Wave to the flying monkeys (of our minds) as we're off on a journey into the unexplored. We have everything we need and more will be there when we arrive.

So breathe in your circumstances and then breathe in your creativity to affect your circumstances, move things around, blow down some old stories, breathe in the spirit of the stories you want to live in. We are creating our experience around living a life on fire with magic and transformation. All of our realizations, perceptions, and passions come alive in the first step on this journey. Go!

Our Authenticity
The Naked Truth

*"The Truth, The Whole Truth, And Nothing But The Truth,
So Help Me God."*

A fable, written in the late 1800s, told a tale of how Truth and Falsehood went bathing in a lake together. Falsehood emerged first from the water and dressed quickly in Truth's garments. It was said that Truth, who was unwilling to wear the garments of Falsehood, went naked. This is how the saying begetting the naked truth was coined. I see the goddess of Truth just standing there unadorned, self-evident, undisputable, and unvarnished. She is walking back to her home on a warm summer day without a care in the world. Like bare children playing on the beach, happy-go-lucky, self-possessed, totally uninhibited, cares to the wind. Imagine just walking along feeling total relief, the easing of a burden, the release of moods, and the release of distress with the bliss of being unconcerned.

The surrendering of our false fronts, the dropping of the game, the maneuvers, the letting go of all that is not bona fide, leaves us at first vulnerable but then well founded by our solidity. The next step, which takes even more courage than surrendering, is the bravery to be lost, wrong, and out of sorts, while accepting exactly where we are now. To chase the future, its to place the future on a weak foundation. To honor an inspired future, is to deal with the now while being enamored with your future dream. How exhausting, always trying to catch up to the program while our inspiration has gone to a party with our passion and left us home because we got lost in a labyrinth of mind matters that were going nowhere. Confusion is the flash of not knowing and a ticket to figuring something out. In the process of finding, retrieving, and releasing our genius, we are in our own world where all expressions of who we are have a place at our table. We play dress up as we are hosting the many aspects of our personas, our style, our social allure, our auras, even down to the way we walk; we are designing ourselves into the beauty of our own uniqueness.

My grandmother Luvy, was a fifties glamour goddess. She lived to be over a hundred and taught me how to dance the cha-cha. She was quite comfortable in her own skin and could care less what people thought about her. A great role model, she had an edge and had no qualms about sliding along on it. Her rebel nature stirred things up, made things saucy, and challenged others to be wild with her.

Luvy was completely enamored with herself, she was the cat's meow dressed to the nines in sparkling gold jump suits, spiked heels, hot pink lipstick, double black lashes, and kitten eyeliner. A self-made millionaire back in her day, her great success came from stuffing the foam rubber my grandfather manufactured for card-table covers into her bra. Luvy had invented what was then called the falsie. A silk-covered piece of foam rubber that slid into a brassiere making women look like Jane Russell bombshells. Then came the Sixties and women's liberation. Luvy was shocked that women were burning their bras; she thought those hippy chicks were crazy and looked like dirty rats. (I was one.) Luvy would always give me tidbits of her philosophy on how to treat a man, which I ignored. "Treat them like they're kings, serve them, make them think they're heroes, then they'll do anything for you." Her advice was simple: Cherish what you love.

I learned the essence of self-love from my grandmother. She cherished herself as if she were a queen and sometimes she was a queen with a bad mouth, she cussed like no tomorrow. Then again, she was not posing to be anything other then her vampy self, a woman who said what she thought, did what she wanted, and felt darn good about herself. She loved to gamble, to dance, and to dress as if everyday was a gala event. She had a scarlet air with a genius mind, if you messed with her she became a tigress, and if you loved her she was your guardian. She taught me the art of loving my wild nature and believing in miracles.

Who decided we had to hone it down? We are limitless beings, allergic to preconceived notions, averse to having to position ourselves, disinclined to exhausting manipulations, and dead-end expectations held by the masses. Our nature is the opposite; we just really want to go out and play with whom we are. We have a total right to just express ourselves. To step into the power of *"I am that–I am."* To be that, we contemplate, sense, experience, and address ourselves. We might sob, shriek, fall apart, and let the emotions that have been held back for so long rise and release. We are unfolding into our great dance and these gyrations may be wild and static, or smooth and peaceful, they are never one-way. In this millennium we are on a journey of profound recovery from the status quo, the greed factor, the chemical imbalances from bad structured food and pollution. We are escaping from money rage, religion rage, and just plain energetic rage. This is a lot to recover from, so yes, be edgy, carry out your passion, learn from your undertakings, and be proud of yourself because you are a survivor and most importantly: your integrity and authenticity have embedded power to support your real truth.

Our inner source is the seed of dreams, our holy land, our unvarnished veracity. It's more important to know the naked truth then to defend a story. The truth needs nothing other than to be as it is. You can't manipulate a truth, or twist it around; it exists beyond words and is felt. As beings, we unfold like a lotus that grows in the mud. So don't turn away from what is tarnished when there is something else under the grime. We need to sit in the mud, to let it gush through our fingers like children who don't worry about their clothes, so we can feel all the things in our hearts in order to know what will heal or hurt us. As children, we learned to tie our shoes before running out, now we are learning that our feelings are the compass dial on the Richter scale of what drives us.

Our successes are not about the end results, they are about the journey, being at peace with it, trusting, and loving it; this lets us own the end result now. If you are not comfortable, strip down, take off what itches, what is too tight, what is not your right color. As we take off our camouflage, and put down our shields, we are exposed. Without our titles, our credits, and the whole brouhaha of who we think we are, we might feel lost. Being lost is the first step on the great adventure of finding ourselves. When we step out of our comfort zone, we might find that maybe we were not really so comfortable there. Comfort is another illusion—it's not sustainable.

We came here to rock our own worlds; so perfect facades, old assumptions, and dull perceptions, will not hold up once things start shaking. We are quaking out of our old precepts into the actualization that we need to access new beginnings. Yes, this is a challenge and yes it calls for us to take the action of stripping away what does not represent us. By doing this we must un-design the imitation we agreed to be and become the original. Our originality undoes the concept of pretend perfectionism. We are already exactly ideal—can we own that? Imagine living with this concept as a baseline. So we agree with ourselves, how does that feel in the midst of being told that what we are doing is wrong? It feels right! External perfectionism and status have a life range of about a month to a few years, tops. Our passion has a lifetime guarantee.

Mentally our minds are geared to follow their own directives of *do what is easy*. Easy is not always the correct path; there are times we must go into the jungle with a machete to cut through new pathways. We must get dirty and sweaty while breaking down old walls; it's not a pristine job. But it's a powerful assignment to break down what is not good enough and get to the source of what is. We have to do this because we become what we surround ourselves with. We are a work in progress and at the same time we are perfect in the now. So how about being okay with who we're not, and letting it be okay that we are in a process of arriving to who we are, and everything on the way is perfectly part of the process. And at the same time we own the fact that we are already perfectly there—this is liberation.

Trusting the universe is a reflection of being able to trust yourself. So maybe if things have not yet worked out, if they are even falling apart, maybe we just are losing what is not good enough and we need to trust that. Take your ego on a fire-walk and let it burn to ash. Rub some on your third eye and say goodbye to self-pride. Tell your old self that you came here to be exactly who you are right now and then tag yourself as it. It's ultimate liberation to walk out of our roles, off the stage and just go home.

The day after 9/11 and in complete shock, I was channel surfing, looking for some semblance of hope and came upon The Daily Show, with Jon Stewart. Curious as to what in these distraught times, this fellow could possibly offer as a way of relief. I was floored as he proceeded to display his genuine anguish on national television. He described himself hiding under his desk in a fetal ball as he watched the destruction. He revealed his pain, love, and undying faith for our country that had been attacked. He was literally sobbing his heart out right on the air. This man was totally vulnerable exhibiting exactly what we all felt. It made me feel safer that he had shown himself this way to become a role model for being authentic.

Many times we think having courage is about being strong, but there are times when it's about being vulnerable and revealing our hearts. It's about showing our cards and being honest, this is what is most healing. When we become straightforward, it creates a space for others to also do so. When suffering and pain arise, we can see the actual wound. It is only then, that we can put on the salve and sanctify our healings. Really as far as our self-healing goes, we are wading through experiences to understand them. When we don't get to the other side of them they are left as unfinished business and as they sit on the back shelves they start to collect mold and rot. Energetically, mold and rot can be considered as shame and guilt. Shame is the consciousness of something dishonorable, a disgrace. Shame is best friends with guilt, who loves to hang out with Pride. This tribe stirs up pain for us. If we really look in the mirror and accept the fact that we all have a side that is not the fairest of them all, that we can be the witch, the mean bastard, the one who curses out car windows and loses it, then we are dealing with real. We must own our nasty side, the things we've done that we don't feel good about—sometimes we have to wade through the swamp where the alligators lurk to get to our other shore.

Hopefully we are not so lost that we can't understand what it is that we do, that is unintelligent. It's our own discernment between who we believe we are and who we are beyond that, that holds our act-fact. Our entire story is not to be authenticated by the judge or the jury; we face our own consequences and deal with what we have to clean up. To understand our pain, we learn it's not endless pain but a pain that takes us across to our heartland. I used to consult healing advisors until I realized my most potent advisor is the universe, and my sense of spirit, which lives in my heart. We can travel to Mongolia, the Amazon, the moon, seeking magic, or we can sit still and go inward to the brimming well of our wisdom and retrieve the magic from there. We are our own diagnostic faith healers who have all the answers within. We can't avoid pain and hardship and in the same sense we should not desert our inside track even as we travel it's badlands, because we are going somewhere important— into our absoluteness.

A real diamond, encrusted in dirt, once discovered, cuts glass. Real truth divulges all distortions; it levels towers of dishonesty and plows down fields of low-level behaviors that need to be recycled. Truth doesn't stop exposing all that is deceptive until it gets to the core of genuine. Once we arrive at the axiom of ourselves, we become our own best friend. Friends accept the good and the bad about each other. There are times I have to accept what is disheartening, what feels unfair, and mentally work on aspects of what it is in me that I need to bring light to. To know we are good and doing our best is to be complete as we are. To feel the wealth of our graciousness allows the universe to match this earnestness.

Our authenticity walks out in front of us like an usher with a flashlight. It's funny that people think they are not obvious when they are totally transparent. Our faces reveal all there is to know about us. Our body language tells our entire story, besides, our vibration always enters the room before we do. We always notice when someone's presence shrieks for attention; they are quietly loud with loads of pretense. At the same time when our authenticity comes forth it shines.

The universe does not support pretense for very long so it will send in a catalyst to take it down. Madame Truth stands in the corner cackling when we are putting on our pageantry. She is planning some great tricks for as we are putting on a grand show and tap dancing across the stage. Madame Truth is quietly oiling our soles, (our souls), so we slip and lose our trumped up standing. Question if every time you fall off your high horse, how were you not in sync with what was needed? Usually we are not centered. Being centered is not a still point it has movement—being off center is going too far in any direction. Everything that opposes harmony is an act of taking something too far. Then again falling out of center is part of how we learn to balance ourselves—we fall and we come back. It's when we fall too far from center, and too hard, that we went too far and then have to heal.

Mr. and Mrs. Ego, the other undermining catalysts who always mind our business, are total control freaks. They have an opinion about everything and at the same time, they're always pretending they are doing what's best for us. In truth, they are greedy, selfish, condescending, and really good at scaring us. As the great authors of all our: Oh-my-God what-if scenarios, that are total traps; this team's agenda is very unbalanced—they think they are the tarot-card holders of our destiny. Wrong! Grab the cards back as our ego's rant is a projected distortion. Even when the odds are against us, we must invest in our heartfelt actuality. So step over the cracks in your mind that say otherwise and keep going. Know that the state we hold today is what we are emanating our tomorrows from.

I once had an astrology reading from a woman who kept telling me how I should be and what to feel. She told me potentially where my destiny was, which was pretty amazing, but she had no tolerance for the process of my arrival. I took the best from the reading but realized that if the universe is a mirror that constantly sends us Morse code messages in communications and activities, I too needed to have more tolerance for my process. Granted, being optimistic is one thing, but being Hallmark perky is not very interesting and basically another lie, especially when one has spent some serious time as a member of a dark underground gang doing shadow-work and having relations with Lord Pluto, the ruler of the underworld.

Pluto's name in Greek also means riches and wealth; therefore, even in the lower world of Pluto's domain there are jewels to be retrieved. As the Greek myth is told, King Pluto kidnapped Persephone and her mother Demeter went nuts looking for her, when Demeter found out where she was, in an underworld with this brute, she demanded her daughters return. Demeter, who was also the Goddess of Harvest and Fertility, was so angry that until her daughter was returned, she stopped the growth of crops, and famine plagued the earth. Finally Zeus, Persephone's father, the Ruler of the Heavens, got involved and sternly demanded Persephone's release, but she had been charmed and had fallen in love with Pluto. Haven't we all once fallen for a Pluto? He agrees to release her for half the year but she must always return to him like the seasons. So our time in our underworlds making love with our shadows is most reasonable when done in an enlightened sense, as this is where we actually make peace with ourselves and transform.

We all have a place of torment, though when called to an inner management meeting with our dark side, understand that we have been called aside by spirit to step beyond there. We are being called to fall into ourselves beyond all the veneers to the source of our beauty. We must scrutinize and review who we are, and disregard who we are not. Here, we go into our wounds, designate the pain, figure out where the inner child is hiding, have a chat with spirit, converse with our darkness, and explain to it that its horn has pierced our heart. This is our time to commune without words—it's time to just howl.

When we recover ourselves by going on this indigenous journey and delving into our unschooled unaffected domains, we return to a natural state of awe. To face oneself completely, dark side and all, is an initiation into our hoarder room where we hid the bags of junk we did not need. Now we will go through them, remembering why we collected each thing in order to disseminate the root of the emotion that needed it. When we get rid of what is no longer serving who we are now, and what we believe in, we are not bothered over what others think about us, we say no without guilt, make mistakes without shame, and we don't keep apologizing for things we aren't sorry about. We no longer do what we think is right, we do what we feel is right. We speak the uncensored lingo that comes from the core of our being, we act upon what we know and frolic in the wilderness of our untamed heart. We have to do this over and over because we are constantly growing out of ourselves.

Every time shadow mind sends in overcast thoughts, this signals the ding that we are up for a confrontation. To choose safety over adventure is to ignore the signal, as we must dare to take on the wager to risk everything for our sanctity. If we want to reach a place where we can just put our duplicity down and be real; we need to allow a space for it to be so. At a certain point it must become a priority to set the stage to enjoy our poetic freedom. We can't wait for it to be handed to us; we must take it for ourselves. Therefore, this deed of self-honor will lead us to walk in truth, speak our truth, seek and recognize the truth, as this dedication is the only risk worth taking. Our adoration of our complete self is our leading act, which takes us out of the rat race and delivers us to lay down naked and rest on a bed of roses.

Reflection:

Imagine yourself as a child that has run away and like a tracker you are going out to find yourself. You sense your presence and finally you see the small version of you, out there all alone, maybe in the woods by a tree, or hiding in a basement, or maybe floating in the clouds, or even hanging out with the stars in the sky. You go to this small version of yourself and acknowledge the reason of why you left. You sit with yourself and honor the reason, and then you tell yourself that you are safe, that all is well, that you will take care of everything, and that you are bringing yourself home. You take this child into your arms, embracing them, and holding them close to your heart, you feel their love melt into yours. You are now complete!

Forgiveness
Our Amnesty

Forgiveness is the fragrance that the violet sheds
on the heel that has crushed it
— Mark Twain

What if you hurt me and I let you get away with it? You did something so inexcusable, so filled with betrayal, that it caused me severe pain. My immediate response was to get back at you, to tell everyone, and to make you suffer the way you made me. Striking back, that's what I always do, but today when you damaged me I went to my corner, curled into a ball, and felt every millimeter of the pain. I then called forth my ambulatory angels and together we healed the wounds. Looking back at you, all I saw were aspects of an old version of myself that no longer existed.

Human beings have done horrible things to each other over the millennia. We have jousted with power, withdrawn love, and imposed hatred. People play with malice, deceit; they have abused, raped, murdered, and tortured each other. On smaller scales, lesser injustices like gossip and self-centeredness can seem like normal acceptable behaviors.

Cheating, lying, and manipulating others, are all nuances we might tell ourselves are undoubtedly admissible because everyone else does it. This is just an excuse, a slip-slide into a mindset that makes up rules based on convenience instead of virtue. We all experience relationships with others in the reactionary group of you poke me; I poke you back—harder. All we are doing in this habitual game is trying to win, but really there is nothing worthy of winning here. Even when we are in the midst of a painful situation we must decide if we chose to invest in anguish, or if we chose to invest in trusting the universe to shift us so we can get what we need and move on.

Overall, none of us ever escape heartbreak, sadness, and life-threatening challenges. As a whole, we've experienced every horrific level of mental, emotional, and physical suffering that has ever existed; we have witnessed Hell in our lifetimes. Hell is not some place we are going to, in fact Hell is happening right here, right now. To compensate for being in Hell, what we must find some beauty that is alive for us and hold onto it for our dear life, as this is how we transverse Hell.

In alternate realities, everything exists at the same time, so there is a dichotomist bond, two opposing classifications that can be married, therefore Heaven and Hell may exist simultaneously. In the same sense that we have good and bad moods, days, and years, our levels of suffering speak to us, they are asking us to become heroes, because that's what we need to be in order to survive such pain. The word hero is defined as a being of superior courage and fortitude. It has been said in a classical Greek myth that a hero is regarded to be the offspring of a mortal being and a God. In my out-there philosophy, this is not too mythical or far-fetched, as it is a fact that we've all basically arrived here from another dimension. We came into human form, live and direct, from spirit form. Honestly only a hero would take this crazy journey, especially at a time like this when the challenges on this planet are herculean, when the world is on the brink of disaster, when greed and apathy are on the welcome committee, and when our presence is sincerely needed to do something about it. We came here to give the best part of ourselves out into this world—and why would we do that? Because this is the greatest gift we can offer. By doing this we are sharing our spark of light.

In the opposite sense, we have shared much darkness with each other in our disagreements, our anger, our mistrust, and our me-first-attitude, all this in the name of survival. The balancing out of this dichotomy revolves around if we can maintain a peaceful state under insensitive circumstances. Can you still hold yourself up in the face of being cut off, cheated, dishonored, destroyed by illness, and a witness to war and torture? Think about it, we lose it all the time over rudeness, which is nothing in the face of hatred, violence, or madness. Losing it is when insanity has cut the connection to our good will. Forgiveness is the action that sets us free. On the one hand, we practice forgiveness because it's the right thing to do. On the other hand, it's about the willingness to let go of all that will never suffice to uplift us—we let go for our own good.

Is it human nature to forgive? Probably not, because look at the state of the world, if everyone constantly forgave, it would be a different atmosphere. The question is do we forgive because we are holy beings who thrive on this lifestyle, or because we know better? Living in pain with anger quietly kills us, while forgiveness is a survival panacea. The challenge to forgive others that are dishonorable, short sighted, selfish, and basically downright unevolved, forces us to come to terms with ourselves. Coming to terms with ourselves is to look in the witch's mirror to see that we also are not the fairest of them all, for when our inner bitch comes out, we go to Hell, and we take everyone connected to us, with us. To impose harmony into hatred forces hatred to change form. This is what we are being challenged to do— change form—mostly our own. The question is how do we trust in something better than what exists when all Hell is breaking lose? If you know how to read energy, all situations are like etheric braille that is talking to us. Sometimes the energy field is blatantly telling us it's time to leave, or we must bypass our emotions to reach a level of peace; it's about maintaining our balance.

Every act we perform and every thought we think pertains to balance. When the scales tip towards negativity there is a shift, which angles towards the turning point of a crisis mode. We oppose this dynamic by holding a more uplifting creative influence. Granted, it is not always easy, and where we become heroes, is by knowing the concept that easy or not easy is going to be thrown to the wayside by virtue of the fact that we are doing whatever it takes. We maintain our position and this position becomes the director of what we do.

A situation that I was banking on to support me fell apart as the party on the other side had no integrity. I was angry that I had lost something I invested in. The initial thought that came to mind was that I was being blocked to advance and put off track. I then had the realization that magic arises when we can see perfection. I saw that I was never comfortable working with this team and there was really nothing magical for me in that project to begin with. I was not being blocked; it was just a stopover where my flight was canceled because I was going in the wrong direction. This was a great turning point and a crucial moment of understanding that I was not aligned with my original purpose. To be aware that many of our difficulties are wake up calls is to forgive the situation and take the best from it. It's as if we got side-tracked and went unconsciousness for a while, and then the truth came to kiss us and we woke up. The gift of seeing the truth as we wake up is like ambulatory assistance arriving with oxygen when we can't breath. When I saw the truth about the greedy types I was doing business with, my first thought was get away, my next thought was to know that it was a low-level consciousness and all I needed to do was raise mine to move on.

We are a karmic clean up crew, like those Pac Men in the video game eating up the exploding bombs. We are the balancers who can stand in tree pose, maybe wobbling or falling over while others are lying, fighting, stealing, and creating non-stop animosity. Negative energy manifests further unfavorable accumulations of disadvantageous patterns. Dark energy builds up, reaches critical mass, and creates an energetic bang that has a tumultuous charge and affects us like the weather. One minute it's sunny, and the next, a storm rolls in. We were on our way to the party, while momentarily we where going one way when an unexpected dark energy permeated the air affecting us, and suddenly we are off following the scent of our raging emotions and we end up in the mud. We don't notice we're in the mud due to its familiarity and owing to the fact that maybe we've lived in it on and off for years so it feels normal. It's not normal, and a house built of mud will not hold up in a storm.

Consider the power of anger; it's so powerful it can take down a mountain. Now put the anger aside and just think about the power it has and what else you can use it for. Our inventive poetic energy is magnetic; its frequency engages what it needs to complete itself. The question to focus on is, what operating system are we functioning on and why? When we come from the vital goodness of natural kindness, we are operating at the highest level. Meanwhile, the dark side exists and is constantly talking to us, enticing us to react to what others do that is not right. We feel vengeance, mixed with the opportunity to gain satisfaction and we crave the pleasure of seeing someone writhe for what they've done to us, it's our nightly cocktail. Witnessing this demise is so addictive that we delight when we see total strangers who've never done anything personally to us, get it good. Some of us are like a lynch mob, following other people's stories through friends, on the news, anywhere we can, to see who's getting it next. In the old days crowds went to watch hangings; it's never stopped. It was Gandhi who said, "An eye for an eye makes the whole world blind."

In the Hindu tale of the *Ramayana*, an epic poem about the battle of good and evil, Rama the great warrior God, was battling Ravana, the most powerful demon that existed. Every time Rama cut off one of Ravana's many monstrous heads, another grew back. Rama finally prayed to the Sun God, to help him conquer Ravana, he then remembered that he had a magical arrow and used it to finally kill the demon king. He could not kill this demon in the same old way; he had to reach beyond his normal reality. The demons that we are doing battle with are not the ones out there in the world but the ones inside ourselves that are geared to take us down. We are constantly slaying their aspects, but they are clever and tricky and like Ravana they keep sprouting new negative aspects. It is when we finally come at them skilled from a higher dimension that they are finally vanquished out of our holy domains.

To be liberated in this lifetime is not necessarily to sit as the great Buddha, but to be free from all that is not our pure honorable state of being. It takes supreme mindfulness to hold an enlightened state; we don't just wake up one morning as saintly beings. We have to do the work of overcoming our darkness and nevertheless even after we have conquered all the low level aspects of ourselves, we still have to continually hold our own. In a state of balance we are rooted into the equipoise of our true source and at the same time we still waver. Mastery is being able to show up for the worthy pain and being practiced enough to stand back from an unworthy pain that does nothing good and wants to destroy us. A worthy pain is the pain that comes from the loss of love, to deny this pain would also mean to deny the love. In time the pain fades but the love never fades—it is ours forever.

An alternative remedy for a corrective panacea is to keep pulling yourself farther away from the distress until you see the larger picture. For instance, go to a museum and stand right up against a painting so your eyes are at most two inches away and all you see is the color blue. Then back away two inches until you begin to see the red next to it. Step a foot back and you might see a flower. Two feet back and you will see a field and five feet back you notice a man on a horse in the distance. You then sit down on a bench and from that angle you notice geese are flying past the man. There is a story going on, but at first all you saw was blue.

In the red zone our psyches are engorged with anger and obscured from compassion. Blinded by these feelings, we are myopic, an intolerance that attracts further contrary dynamics towards us. The antidote is to reverse our mindsets and observe the other side of what exists. There is always an alternative choice to reasoning, another side of the coin, an alteration—the flip side. Mastery teaches us how to move an energy field but firstly we direct our ego to step aside and secondly, we call for our witness so we can see what is worth seeing. The witness expands our perceptions. Thirdly, we then anchor into any level of certitude we can muster up, we hold onto goodness, we define want we want beyond what is and shift into it. We are in control of where we are going, what we are thinking, and ultimately how we are feeling. Mastery puts us in our power and once there the low-level game is over because we're not playing.

The most elevated action is to oppose feeling stuck in adversity. If we can send love to a person who is enraged and attacking, this will neutralize and stabilize us back to whom we really are, therefore the negativity coming at us may no longer bend us the wrong way. Sending love towards healing a negative situation is the highest countenance we can do for our own healing. This highest most evolved conduct is the action that protects us.

The one who insolently holds back boiling mad, acting stubborn, and thick skinned, is foolishly relinquishing their abilities to become the hero. When we step forward first, we are doing it to elevate ourselves out of damaging situations. It really doesn't matter whether the forgiveness is accepted, what matters is that we forgave and opened our hearts so we're not shut down and stuck in someone else's bad dynamic, which is energetic vampirism. In the same sense that a sealed jar preserves food for the long haul, we are preserving our good frequency to help us hold our own in the face of adversity.

Helen Keller's teacher, Anne Sullivan, taught Helen, who was blind, the meaning of words with love and patience because it fulfilled her. Young Helen was wild and defiant, her family supported this, but Anne Sullivan demanded adherence to her format of teaching Helen. Ms. Sullivan removed Helen from her normal surroundings and continued spelling constantly in Helen's hand until a spark was transmitted. Removed from her normal surrounding gave Helen no other choice but to learn. Helen described the exact moment she understood her teacher was spelling in her hand. She said, *"After I stood still, my whole attention fixed upon the motions of her fingers. Suddenly I felt a misty consciousness as of something forgotten—a thrill of returning thought and the mystery of language was revealed to me. I knew then that W-A-T-E-R meant the wonderful cool something that was flowing over my hand. That living word awakened my soul, gave it light, hope, joy, set it free."* Helen Keller then came forth as an advocate for the blind, the poor, and all women.

I bring this up as a point to never give up on people, never walk away when your heart needs to stay, show up and do what needs to be done—no matter what. Helen Keller also said, *"It is wonderful how much time good people spend fighting the devil. If they would only expend the same amount of energy loving their fellow men, the devil would die in his own tracks of ennui."*

Everything going on that opposes our evolved dynamic always comes back to the fact that we are not following our amplified goodness. We cannot live our lives hiding while trying to avoid mishaps and pain, nor can we control the way others behave towards us. The only protection we have is to create peace. This way when the dregs show up, they can't get to us because we are not in their dirt heap. So don't hook into negativity, don't listen to it, and keep your focus on the goodness you want to hold in your heart. Hold the state you wish to live in over everything else. Notice how you relate to the stories going on, do you allow yourself to become triggered by them, or do you delve into them and then process them out when they bring up issues? We balance darkness in ourselves when we spotlight it. Witnessing what we grow in the shade makes very obvious what aspects we are holding onto that need light. We must stop trying to fix the same things over and over, and just fix what is broken in ourselves. The truth is we can shift any storyline—mentally. A great writer is not afraid to throw an entire manuscript in the trash and start again.

A vicious cycle is where we keep casting old stones, as opposed creating new stories. So every time you feel bad, challenge it, and every time dark feelings take you away from your bliss, bring them down. Intercept grim feelings around every corner, cut them off in every argument, shortstop them the moment a bad wish or intention arises. Every time we react, fight back, or gossip, we lose power and will remain powerless until we realize our true power emanates from a peaceful state. We need to acknowledge that we all have a dark side and send constant love and light to it, otherwise it becomes a self-righteous dark side, or an in-denial dark side that is hard to penetrate.

The difficult relationships we are having out there are an opportunity to offer healing to ourselves. Our attitude affects how we feel about ourselves, so when bad feelings come up, stop everything, and consider the end result of what you are doing. In this way, we are serving our highest self by doing what serves our highest good in the end. A man I was doing business with taught me about honor and where my true power is. I had worked tirelessly with him, investing my time, my money and sweat equity, towards the goal of selling his property. As we got near the finish line it became obvious that this man had no appreciation for my work at all. He could care less about me, was just a user, and basically a villain. I saw long patterns of this kind of selfishness in my business equating to one word: Greed.

My first impulse was anger, which I struggled to not act upon, but it won out. I was raging about the injustice of it all; furious, and railing it out with no holds barred. Finally, calling out to my guides I prayed for support, which brought me into an inner dialogue about the reason for this experience. In that moment my rage became like an inner wash cycle, that just rolled through and dislodged something—my belief in this storyline. Seeing this brought me to a sacred space where I was able to let go and be free of emotion and from there I asked my guides to show me where the honor in any of this was. In that moment everything stopped, there was shift because I had pulled out of my railing dynamic to earnestly request knowledge, so the door to higher knowledge opened. A light went on as I saw myself as a warrior on a cliff with a sword yelling to the clouds, "Show me jealousy, show me regret, and please show me honor."

After urgently requesting to be shown honor, I saw clearly that this characteristic lived inside me in the fact that I was a being struggling to rise above my lowest feelings for this trickster man. So perhaps the man was not honorable but that was not enough to change the fact that I was. The gift I received that day was that I recognized it in myself. The image of this creepy man faded and I saw the return on my investment not in dollars but in a lesson that taught me about the tribute I held inside myself. I saw that my return was in the fact that I was the one who had integrity and it would carry me.

Animosity is a trick, a thief among thieves who robs our most divine power, which is love, and throws it in the garbage. My mother and her sister had a fight. No one in my family even remembers what it was about. My mother reached out so many times for her elder sibling but my aunt would not forgive. On her deathbed my mother called out again and again for her sister. She never came, never called, not a letter or even a flower was sent. I wanted to scream

"Wake up!" at the top of my lungs but all I could do was wake up for them.

Many times we learn the hard way. I learned about the after-effects of false power from my friend Ms. Karma, who arrived one day to harshly shake me up and teach me about illusions. Ms. Karma took me on quite a painful journey, an initiation, which created a dynamic of nothing working unless it had integrity. False power has zero integrity, nor does spiritual materialism. This painful journey took me apart and gave me no other choice but to put myself back together in a new way, a higher more evolved way. Our inner confrontations demand an about face when they need to be acknowledged. It's a painful blessing to not escape our low-level shenanigans that create bad karma. Our most potent teacher is the consequence of our own actions, pushing us to work them out. This awareness immediately brought me home to my power place and completed the healing I needed.

I recently learned a great lesson from a stubborn person who refused to work out a miscommunication with me. It is in the times we feel cheated, bullied, and bamboozled that the gift of self-examination is most useful. It pushes us right to the mirror to find what within ourselves is off kilter and needs love. Letting go of grievances is at the top of the list, being the victim is next; these dynamics have no right to define us. To illuminate ourselves beyond vindication, we must reach for the insight of love. Reasoning does not work here, only the heart works. The heart has tenacity and will beat through every idiom our mind makes up. It is our heart that knows when to step away from anger and disappointments, it knows when to empower us to move away from what doesn't work. Our great heart is the keynote speaker of our being and knows when it's time to call out for a healing of all that's hurting us. This great heart will lead us into doing all that needs to be done to alleviate our pain. The heart is a vessel that travels the most robust seas of life, it never gives up beating it's drum of love until the day it is done, and then it takes us with it into new realms. The nature of hearts is for giving.

Reflection:
Observe a negative story as if it were a mental hologram. Pretend the hologram is like a crystal ball and ask the hologram if what is going on is valid; you will get an immediate inner answer. Ask for the underlying reasoning, ask for all that you need to know to be revealed, ask what it will take to transmute this dark story so you can change all the stenciled dynamics. Just in the act of construing these requests, you are changing the paradigm around you, disrupting a fixed arrangement of a theme, and recreating a new framework. We came here to evolve, so forgive yourself, forgive others, excuse them, pardon, absolve, and make amends; it's all we can do and all that is needed. There is infinite mercy in the fact that we are guests here, doing what we do and having all that what we have.

We must be gracious to our host, this wondrous planet that allows us free rein in her playground and has offered us so many gifts. We return the gift by embellishing all that holds goodness—no matter what.

Love Rules
Our Heart's Seal

"Only words and conventions can isolate us from the entirely undefinable something which is everything." –Alan Watts

Welcome to love's lessons this is a lifelong course, there's no signing in–just arrive. We're all here on celestial scholarships so there are no fees or velvet ropes. Take off your shoes; put down your bags, you don't need them in this reality. You can close your eyes or keep them open, the cupid of love doesn't care, just don't run away when their arrows of love are piercing your heart.

Love is elusive, running in front of us and hiding, and then sneaking up on us, it pulls so hard on our coattails that we just fall into it. There are no rules or boundaries with love, you can't make it happen or tell it to leave; it runs its own show and calls all the tunes. Love is enamored by our yearnings and seduced by our aspirations. Concrete or illusionary, noble or cautioning, a sign of things to come or a tell-tale moment; we're falling for love no matter what. This tutelage of love bypasses all that is rational, it goes beyond reason and delivers us into a state of enchantment where we are lost in love.

Love is like a tornado with a heart, she pulls us in until we abandon all concepts of separation and give her carte blanche to take us on her journey. She spins us around so we lose the idea of who we think we are and just become love. Lost in love we have no say about our immersions—we are gone. Our devotedness takes us on a karmic journey, which we might think has no rhyme or reason, but it does. A karmic love story is one that must complete itself. So when a love-story makes no sense, it is designed by the fate of the stars—the handwriting of destiny.

When love is karmic, it happens with the same people in different lifetimes so we can finish our lessons with them. For instance, suppose you had a lover to whom you were abusive and it broke his heart, he then went away but he never got over you. This created a karmic bond that manifested an opening for this story to finish itself. Having karma with someone is a sequel that has a beginning, middle, and an ending, or maybe a never-ending. So now your hurt lover has gone on his merry way licking his wounds. You never knew of the fatal car accident or read of his tragic passing because you had lost track of him. Years later you've married someone else and given birth to your first child, a beautiful son.

This little boy is extremely needy, and screams every time you leave the room. He demands to be breastfed constantly. The next thirteen years are turbulent as this child turns you inside out. You are constantly nurturing and bestowing non-stop love on this boy, which seems like it's pouring endlessly down a bottomless hole. Finally, the boy grows up and at a very young age he runs away leaving you in the dust. You weren't prepared as he severed the cord, stating clearly that he no longer needs you, now hates you, and never wants to see you again. Your heart is shattered and broken. Now, imagine the possibility of this beautiful son being the shunned lover returning from his past life to stake a claim in his loved one's heart. Perhaps returning to teach his loved one the searing lesson of a broken heart.

The karmic spell of loving beings we have traveled with many times before is the return of a historic love that greets us again and again. Love, like a radar beam finds us in the storm, then disappears and comes again; it likes to play hide and seek to wake us up. Love is a teacher of consideration and care that challenges us to stay when we are needed and give all that we have. It demands respect and honesty or it will hold itself even higher spouting shiny apples that we have to find a ladder to get to. Many times love will hang around in our ugliest moments covering all the mirrors because looks don't matter. Love only wants what is real.

Love is a teacher that strengthens our soul's connection and brings us into sessions of supreme worship training. Once love gets in, it will continue to flow boundlessly to teach us how to flow that way. It wants us to give all we have so it can replenish our heart. It laughs at our resistance and knocks us over until we surrender. There were times in my life that things were scarce for me and I felt I had nothing left to give. I hid small wads of money in socks under the mattress; it was emergency money. My boyfriend and I were barely twenty years old at the time. Sometimes we had no money to even go to the grocery store and even then I never unveiled the hidden wad of money. To me hunger was not an emergency, having to get away was an emergency, and this money was my escape fund.

One day, my husband to be found my small wad of money buried under the bed and he looked at me like I was crazy. He has always stood by me, shown me I never had to run, and still years into our marriage he has never not relinquished everything he could for my happiness. We still laugh about this because he never held anything back, only I did. My escape fund always kept me distant. What was I prepared to run from besides a lack of faith? Everywhere we go, there we are.

Love demands trust, we are being held by its validity, there is nowhere else to go but deeper into a paradise that is sacred. Sounds like a fairy tale but it's not, try it, practice allowing love in by loving what is around you, an animal, a flower, a dream, a stranger, a book, a song, or a being who has passed and is now a star in the sky. You will find that love exists when you focus on it. A baby is lost in love with itself, and as such, we are all beings who hold undying love in our essence, our spirit, and our heart's domain.

Our supreme essence is none other than complete and total love. Look in the mirror; you are a most heroic passionate soul who came here to be exactly you. As we stand in the perfection of all our imperfections with our arms open to hold hands with ourselves, we find we are the soul mate we've been waiting for. When we fall in love with ourselves, the vault where our treasure exist, opens. So break the rules, abandon your ego at the door and pass through all love's realms and spectrums of emotional tangents. It's amazing what masks we can rip away and how vulnerable we become on behalf of our love for another, but would you do it for yourself? Would you fight that hard for yourself? We can only love another as much as we love ourselves.

A girlfriend was in love with a man who said he couldn't love her back because it wasn't convenient. Everyone she knew tried to talk her away from this man. He was mean, selfish, and lied. My friend tried to shut down her love for him, but it just would not go away. It woke her in the night banging on the door of her heart. So she accepted it and just let herself love this difficult man as he was. She didn't show up for rejection or sadness, just love, and as she moved through her life there was something special about her, something rich warm and attractive because she wasn't bitter or shutdown in her heart. She couldn't be robbed of the love experience, which eventually brought her down a more sacred path to finally love someone who loved her back equally. At the end of this love story she had no regrets because she learned that love is the teacher and she had graduated from a one-sided love affair.

The tales spun of love, encompass all the rocky paths, we stumble, get light-headed, and our heart pounds as we are in the unknown where the oxygen is different. We get to the summit and instead of celebrating, sometimes we lose our balance, our faith, and we fall off the mountain. We crash without parachutes because we couldn't get out hearts open to fly. After our crashes while we are healing, we see where we were not able to glide. We see how much baggage we carried that made us too heavy. Were we really all there? Or were we out of our minds and crazy? We'd push each other's buttons, trigger wound mines, slap our lover's ego in their face, and then we wonder what we did wrong. We are sorry and what is crazier is that we then repeat the process. What's going on is that we have bankrupt stuff in our hearts. We feel empty and can't love up so our mind steps in and tries to fake it. Since we attract back the frequency we are on, our relationships often don't work out, not because they were bad, but because our love sector was empty, it had no fuel, the house was dry.

Love will fade when we have drunk all the remnants in its cup and not replaced it. Some relationships get tired. After the initial euphoria passes it takes genuine skill to prevent our demons from joining us in our sacred soirée. When love slips away, we must at times go to the depths for a rescue, while at other times it's definitively over and we must heal. When it's over we hold the tender memories in our hearts and honor the source from where they came. To pine over a loss of love is a lie, we never owned the source, only the love. The great loves of our lives are in our cells, they are a part of who we are that will exist with us through eternity forever.

An open heart is real; it will tell the truth even when it's painful and it will listen to the truth even when it's hard. The truth travels beyond our distorted voices to its own source. It knows where it's going, has its own reasoning, and reminds us we are just passing through. When we arrived in this world, we were literally cupids just immersed in love. Remember?

We were all once babies floating inside our mother's being, just reveling in the process of our creation. Babies have no concepts; they know no fear and care nothing about considering the beginning or end of existence. Completely delighted in themselves, they participate in every experience fully with no agenda. Everyone adores babies, they are so cute but it's the purity of their unhampered love that we are attracted to and magnetized by. Babies laugh, smile, howl, and shriek to their heart's content. Then they grow up and a million rules and concepts are forced upon them, and piece-by-piece, their original fearlessness and wonderment gets displaced. Suddenly what was once astonishing is no longer allowed. It is totally dumbfounding that a state of stunning intimacy can be shut down as one is forced to conform. This is the turning point where we begin to repress, curb, and inhibit ourselves.

Our suppressed evolution is not natural; we must reclaim it by bringing our magic back. We restore it by falling back in love with ourselves and divining our awesomeness. Revisit all the original turning points where wonderment was lost. Return to your unschooled unaffected domains where you speak your true uncensored lingo coming from your essential core. In a natural state, we say no without guilt, make mistakes without shame, and we don't keep apologizing for things we are not sorry about. We enjoy who we are. We contemplate, we feel, we sense, we address, we may even shriek. We don't question everything, we allow ourselves to just be. We show up for ourselves, we feel what we feel to the depths, as naturally expressive beings are spontaneous. As we reclaim the love we have for ourselves, it flows.

I spent some years sitting at the feet of a meditation teacher who opened and closed all her talks by saying, "With great respect and love I welcome you with all my heart." These were not empty words for she was sitting there seeing the beauty in all beings, and while stern or doting, she was a total vessel for love. Her love was so pure and so solid that it bestowed a transmission. It is impossible to not feel love in the presence of a being that is overflowing with love because love is medicine—it heals everything.

Things are not always as they seem, we are not just mortal beings; we are as magnanimous as the universe itself. Our spirits are attuned to love; they recognize it in a blink because spirits have no preconceived notions. When our spirits soar in the bliss of love, nothing else matters besides the experience. When we have glimpses of this bliss it is only because we have given in and allowed our spirits to take us there. Our spirits every endeavor is to come from love and it's in their every venture to show us. Meanwhile, as we are addicted to getting lost in sensual pleasures, our spirits are attracted to eternal sweetness and getting lost in bliss. When we have glimpses of this bliss it is only because we have given in and allowed our spirits to take us there. We are kings and queens who have majestic spirits that adore us enough to follow us wherever we go, they will never abandon us the way we've abandoned each other and ourselves. Stop pulling away from where your spirit wants to go, follow it like a tracker and you will be led right to the fire pit of love.

Love is our offering; it will bang on the door of our hearts until they open. We did not come here to just pass through, we came for the complete experience, and the taste of all there is. Love is the vein that runs through the essence of all things, so even when love is shut down and tossed away it hangs around, actually there is nowhere it is not because it is inside us.

To open the flow of love pretend that everything that happens is in the name of love. This game shifts ones mind out of judgment and into finding what can possibly be good in what goes on. When we seek for what is favorable, our goods will come forth. Our enchantments exist in our everyday experience and so does our love, so maybe we just begin with tapping our toe in rhythm with the beat of our hearts. We are just getting in sync so we can be swept off our feet by love.

Reflection:

Loving yourself is your constitution and all you can ever really stand on. Our entire existence is our illustration of love. Unravel everything from who did what, to who you think you are, and even who you came here to be, then all you will have left is love. Really, all that matters is that we know we are that. And this is our offering . . .

Meditation:

Recall being a spirit and moving into the being of a baby. If you don't remember then imagine. Your spirit essence is pure love delivered into physical form. Revel in this illuminated state of being pure love. Imagine that you are just floating around in the bliss of love you have for yourself inside the body of another being who adores you. Now, hold that same feeling and sense that you are being held in the womb of the world and nothing has changed, you are still being held in love. The universe is so grateful you have come to play in its field and has surrounded you with love.

Imagine this love touching upon all that you come in contact with, even the people that you do not agree with energetically. Let go of everything that is not sparked with this love and melt into it. Now let it travel beyond your world to go where it needs to go and do what it does. You have just offered a spark of your love to the universe.

Great-full-ness
Our Soul's Delight

"Piglet noticed that even though he had a Very Small Heart, it could hold a rather large amount of Gratitude."
-A.A. Milne, Winnie-the Pooh

It was a scintillating morning, the birds were singing and the sun was shining. New York City was basking in sweetness on a warm September morning. The children were happy to be in their first week of school, it was the beginning of a new season. We moved with certainty enjoying our coffee, walking a little more slowly to enjoy the perfection of the day. But by nine o'clock that morning we'd been slammed to our knees as the day turned to horror and the casual-go-lightly way we lived would never be the same. The days following 9/11 seemed so unreal that it became hard to take anything at all for granted and just the fact that the sun would ever shine again, was a gift.

Billions of hearts across the planet broke that day and all of humanity stepped forward to offer their prayers and their grief. This act of atrocity changed the way we would now live, as paranoia would become the new governor and Big

Brother would be on the lookout. Living in this age of *Kali Yuga*, as described centuries ago in the Indian scriptures as the darkest period before the new dawn, we are being called upon to honor all that is good. Consider this life as akin to an inter-active epic movie, and the goal is to blow through darkness and stand in goodness, this is it—the big turning point—and we're up at bat. To oppose darkness we need to hit our spark of light-filled goodness out of the field and leave a trail of it behind us as we go.

On that heartbreaking September day, a great wave of love also rose up and shined through the darkness to illuminate the stairway to heaven for all the lost victims and heroes. So yes, there were terrorists that day, it was a day from Hell, but we were also reminded that the supreme quality of life would continue to exist no matter what for wherever darkness resides light will always exist alongside. We were reminded again when the Indian Ocean tsunami of 2004 caused horrific and catastrophic devastation and human loss. The level of pain felt was like a howl heard around the world. Again we rushed forward to help others through the sorrow and grief. Children returned Christmas presents and donated money, everyone stepped forward in support, even if it was only with a prayer and a tear. Then the very next year hurricane Katrina hit New Orleans and there was more devastation. The horrific floods created more heartbreak; many homeless families had no food as things there quickly went from bad to worse so we rushed forth again. New York, Haiti, Japan, India, Mexico, and the

Philippines, all over the Earth: mudslides, earthquakes, hurricanes, and typhoons are constantly occuring. When this kind of continual tumultuousness exists, it's impossible to ignore the pain of others, for even if we're numb our psyches still feel every inch of it. It is no longer just happening to them it's happening to all of us.

These more than usual waves of destructive experiences are constantly forcing us into coming forward, repeatedly in union, to comfort and share love. A quantum shift is happening in the universe and this constant flux of upheaval is showing us that where there's pain, there's also healing. At the same time the fighting in foreign countries continues and constantly reminds us that a crazy dark layer of negativity still remains. Yet heaven still prevails, for in the hub of what is sacred, whatever is good can never really be slain. Goodness will always exist and it is our calling to stand in gratitude for it. Beauty abounds in our everyday ordinary routine and is ours for the taking. When we see this beauty and focus on it, we are enhancing its existence.

There is charm in the simple things, the quiet moments, and the things we do that make a difference. To offer a kind hand, an open heart, our consideration, and the ability to just listen; thus in doing so we step beyond ourselves. Moreover, to oppose darkness we slam it with the opposite; we come forth to share good will and generosity. Amazing that a simple smile engages merit and may oppose all the inherent rights and wrongs.

There is an elevator operator in my building that is always beaming. He stands in a box all day, just going up and down with the biggest smile on his face. All day long people get into his elevator carrying their unruly moods with them; his mindset always remains solid because he's infallibly content. His exuberance is contagious. I wondered if he was crazy, sanctified, medicated, perhaps self-trained by Tony Robbins tapes, but in asking him how he's like this he told me he's just grateful for every moment. Whenever I ride with him, whatever impatience I have, or moods I get into that elevator with, seem completely insane compared to his smile. My inner child knows he is really a super hero disguised as an elevator man.

The frequency of this planet has quickened and whatever our focus is placed upon is now manifesting itself at light speed. We are being asked to put ourselves out there by creating new intentions secured in enlightened chains of thought—this is how we now serve. Who and what is it that is pushing us this way? It is the best part of us that is connected in with the best part of the universe—this unity sets the perfect conditions. So when you step out and it's crazy out there with an overload of moods, negativity, unhappiness, and hardship, you have an opportunity to shift it by shifting yourself as you move through it. Imagine passing through a dark tunnel and leaving a trail of light behind you. In order to do this, you must raise your energy field to over-ride what is going on. When lousy things happen, what measures us is how we can transform, firstly our feelings about what's going on, and then to rollup our sleeves to modify the exchange into something else by offering something valuable to it. We are actually just transforming ourselves in response to what exists.

Many years back, all dressed up and on my way to work as a hair and makeup artist for a fashion shoot, I was waving down a taxi one morning in Manhattan when out of nowhere, a flock of pigeons flying overhead explosively shat all at once, all over me. I was covered in bird shit. Time stood still as a group waiting at the bus stop all looked at me and burst into laughter. I totally lost it and as the Britannica of bullshit ran through my mind, I heard it's litany of: "I must deserve this because I am bad, just go home and pretend you're sick, get into bed and hide, those laughing people are hideous, it should be them, this is going to be a day from Hell, my life sucks." Suddenly, in the midst of that entire negative dribble I heard my mother's voice say, "Bird Shit is Good Luck."

Amazing how one good message can pierce a catalogue of lies. I decided to go with my mother's belief and arrived at the photo shoot still covered in bird shit to peals of laughter and everyone helping me to get it off. The art directors were so grateful I showed up that they donated to me some of the designer's clothes to change into and keep. It turned out to be a great day as I had chosen the best option from the menu, "That being covered in bird shit was good luck!"

A woman had written how in a divorce custody battle, she was literally crawling to the court to go before the judge.

In the last moments she had to pull herself up and put on the show of her life in order to not lose custody of her child. She had to walk into the courtroom with confidence and portray a self-contained powerful woman with the capacity to hold serious responsibility. In reality she was broke and ripped to shreds, but in the constant putting on of this performance the universe empowered this act more than her cascading reality. It did so because she was sparking promise. She won the court case and walked out of there into her new four-star production to become a well-known self help speaker and author.

We need to magnify what is good and what works in order to bring more of the same home. Stop seeing the cup half-empty as when our focus is directed on what's not there, our force of attraction becomes like a backward magnet and everything we want is always out of our reach. We can't have what we cannot own. Our thoughts and beliefs are that powerful, as they hold us back or take us across. Even when life throws a powerful punch and knocks the air out of us, it is our state of mind that decides if we are going down or we're going to keep going. Things going on always have a life span. That is unless we keep defining ourselves as being caught up in a pattern as opposed to being part of an evolving life force that can affect a pattern.

To shift an energy field means we are doing what it takes to bring up our lifestyle so we can live in the mode we imagine. Sienna was a fashion model and as she neared the ripe old age of twenty-six, she was full of angst over the fact that her career might be coming to an end. In reality she was still working almost everyday and looked more beautiful than ever, but her mind was living in the demise of what her future could bring. She exercised everyday and ate only healthy food, but this would not be enough to save her. Monkey mind had taken over so she was mentally and obsessively climbing up and down the monkey bars of bad thinking. She needed a distraction, not an escape. She needed to do something that was potent with passion, something challenging, so she went to acting school. Acting had always been her secret passion and by placing her focus on something she adored, she was satiated. Her energy field changed as a result and her modeling career, even at her ripe age, (crazy rules), took off and went to the next level.

The gifts arrive when we proceed from the perspective of being thankful while showing respect and honor for everything that serves us. The law of appreciation in its very essence has the spark to create more attraction. It's a skill to shift our perspectives to how good things are. If you can't find the silver lining, you aren't looking in the right way. Our expectations of how and when our desires bear fruit, blows out our wish fulfilling candles. Funny that when our desires take a while, many times we just drop it and are on to the next thing. So then how important is it? When it's mandatory we don't give up. We have faith and understand that it's taking time because the universe is making it better prior to sending it. Meanwhile we get ready, so open a new bank account, even if you just have a dollar to deposit, you are depositing good energy into an account with your name on it.

A friend who has her own television show and publishes many books on lifestyles and entertaining, decided she wanted to be paid a an exorbitant amount of money for her next book contract. Her agent laughed and told my friend this was impossible, and then dropped her as a client, saying she could never make her happy. My friend got more rejections from other agents and even though there was contentious doubt hanging around, she held steadfast to her vision because she felt in her bones that it was possible. Finally, at a dinner party, she met a new agent and told him her plan; he was the first to not jinx her wish, he made no promises but said that he would try. Within two weeks he had a bidding war going between two major publishing houses. Lo and behold, he got her a major advance on a series of lifestyle, entertainment, and culinary guides. Granted it was a series of four books, not just one book, but she saw it as an expanding book, which was even better than her original vision.

When people complain over and over about their precious problems, they're locking themselves in with them. They are aligning with all the things that they don't want, so their energy field runs parallel with what's wrong and what doesn't work—then nothing works. While describing and obsessing on our issues, we keep our troubles close by continually painting their portraits. These crummy stories capture us and then become the same old story, which is not the story we want. People constantly describe all the rules of the storyline they are running and from their descriptions they have drawn a map showing where they have been captured and held hostage. When I tell them that they can erase that part of the map and change the story, that they can be the exception, many times they argue, defending their concept of "This is how it is in the real world." I tell them that it's just how you believe it is and I leave them with that.

The real world is described as something existing as fact: not imaginary. Something that exists aside from the idea that created it. Reality is a strange concept because it is totally created by ideas. In a real world everything has an objective existence, but how real can it be when nothing is how it will be forever? It reminds us of the nature of impermanence. All that we can count on is what exists inside us: our life force, our passion, and our gratitude. To honor our quality of life is to have appreciation for our existence. Even if we've been knocked down and all we can hold on to is a fast breath, we are still here, and have to do something with that. Responsively, as long as we can take a breath, we can inhale an inspiration, play with imaginative animation, and live on an implication. Our inner world creates who we are in the real world—it is a real world.

Consider an objective lens, it's the lens in a microscope that receives the rays from an object and forms an image. So if we look at something through an objective lens, we are seeing what can be seen beyond the human eye, supposedly what really exists. To know our quality of life, we also go beyond what we think exists to what is essential underneath that. Our quality of life is about investing in personal satisfaction, investing in the way we live no matter what occurs on the outside. When we feel gratitude we are honoring what is pleasing. If we can find what is pleasing, agreeable, and gratifying, even while sifting through the dirt, we own our pleasure. Once we possess this feeling, it can't be taken away unless we lose it, then we must feel for it and get it back.

We use the mind to deal with external things, to function, to operate, to maneuver. We use the mind of the heart to breath in life force and grow dreams. When we reach a place of commitment with who we are, what we want, and what we do, we own our freedom. So with the freedom we have to be any which way, doing any desired thing, when we know that the feeling we want in the end is gratitude then everything we do in the middle is aligned with our end result.

Katie, a friend who is at a powerful turning point that scares her to the bones, always says, *"It's all good"* after every difficult episode she describes going on. By verbalizing this power statement at the end of her difficulties, she is affirming there is still good there. Katie has no idea where she's going but she knows where she is ending up. Even as Ms. Katie is driving from one end of America to the other in a U-Haul with her dog and all her stuff, she knows it's going to be all good at the end of the day because in her mind that's all there is to it.

Many times we are brought to our knees in pleading or prayer, but how many times have we kissed the ground in gratitude? Maybe after a scary plane ride has landed safely, we think about kissing the ground, but by the time we get to the baggage claim we have forgotten about it. How many times did we not recognize that there was anything to be thankful for until something terrible came to slap us and we realized how good things were? Often we are stuck in our heads traveling into the future worrying about if we will be sick, poor, and lonely, so we gear our lifestyle to make sure it doesn't happen that way. We traveling are on the Anxiety Cruise, traveling through all the what-if horrors trying to keep them at bay, and instead of living to the hilt, we are experiencing stilted living.

The weight of the world is upon us, as we alone perceive ourselves to be the ones holding it all together. How many moments have we missed because we mind-traveled away to a distant low-level memory of say a fight with a loved one, or an experience that went awfully wrong to immerse us in fear and anger? We no longer can hear the birds chirping, the laugher of children that echoes from the park—we are lost. Our bodies are vacant as we are blinded by torrents of uncontrolled thoughts that rob us. When our mental paths are cluttered with jargon and debris, they must be cleared. So when things get difficult, know they've arrived straight from the Universal Fed-Ex because we'd unconsciously ordered them. Return the order and freeze your credit on all unwarranted purchases. Find and focus on the one good thing you can acquisition and if there isn't one, make one up. There is always something available to appreciate even if you are sitting on the sidewalk with your cat and two cents. It could be a perfect cloud in a blue sky, a passing smile, or a cup of coffee. Hold fast to it, it's a lifeline.

If goodness and gratitude were human beings, I see them as lovers walking down the street together enamored with each other and everything around them. Goodness is a deliberate preference and a point of convergence; a meeting place to align and recalibrate our hearts. When we focus on goodness we instantly recognize the hint of a smile, the bliss of a tear, the grace of a cat, the sweetness of a child, and the blessings of a friend. Gratitude is the deep appreciation of goodness. We are the goodness we desire, in our being exists an abundant expanse of beauty, to know it is to see it everywhere. The poet Saint Rumi, wrote, *"Let the beauty we love, be what we do. There are hundreds of ways to kneel and kiss the ground."*

Reflection:
> *"Any fool can be happy. It takes a man with real heart to make beauty out of the stuff that makes us weep."*
> — Clive Barker, *Days of Magic, Nights of War*

Kneel down, place your hands on the floor or the earth, put your forehead to the ground and thank this world for its goodness. Your humbleness is your openness to receive. Go through an entire day using "Thank You" as your mantra. Practice seeing goodness around you no matter what is going on. When you see pain, when you see what is hideous, what is wrong, muster up all the goodness you can foster and send it there. Do it as a practice so when difficult things arrive you immediately think, "Great, now I get to practice." We are channels, and the many acts of our generosity nourish good will. What we nourish is what we keep alive. Being a fool for happiness is favorable and creating beauty is our magic.

Power-Full
Superheroes in Human Form

"Superman is, after all, an alien life form. He is simply the acceptable face of invading realities." — Clive Barker

Christopher Reeve, the late actor who played Superman on film said, *"What makes Superman a hero is not that he has power, but that he has the wisdom and the maturity to use the power wisely. From an acting point of view, that's how I approached the part."* This is such potent wisdom because we all have power and we know from the state of the world that most people do not use it wisely and maturely.

Power not used wisely, ultimately becomes poison. The difference between wise and strong is you can clomp around on strength, show off your muscles, stockpile your bags of gold, but with wisdom you can travel into other realms, you can leave what does not uphold you in the dust, you can create more of what uplifts you, and most importantly, like Superman, you can oppose darkness. We've all done battle with our shadow sides, we've cleaned up their messes and sworn we had it under control when suddenly a triggered emotion erupts and there we are, once again, with our boxing gloves on. Since the opposite of combat is forth-rightness, when we stop fighting with our shadow we then have the ability to consider what it will take to own our darkness. Once we own it, it softens us by bringing up compassion, which is the opposite of anger. To understand everything as being an asset is to be able to use each thing that goes on for all it's worth. For instance, I feel paranoid, someone is gearing up to hurt me, and instead of retaliation I go inside and take my paranoid feeling apart, I let it talk to me, and then I talk back to it, and we come to a place where we agree we are hunky-dory. So I have used this paranoid feeling to step off into something else that satiates me.

Having the consciousness to feel satiated within ones-self takes us out of the false power game. When one is satiated they don't need to do the money dance, the ego strut, the sell-out. Their quality of life serves them well, as they are busy doing what they love. Can we become gratified by our own intrigue and find our goodness even in a dirt heap? The energy field of goodness is like a power switch that works on the same premise as a light switch, as once it's turned on we can see in the dark.

There is an old world parable about Heaven and Hell called, *The Long Spoons*. A young boy asks God to show him the difference between Heaven and Hell. The boy is brought to a large dining hall to see a swell of people with very long spoons siting in front of huge bowls of food. The people are all trying to reach the food to their mouths but their spoons are too long. They are angry, starving, yelling at each other, throwing the bowls, hitting each other with the spoons and destroying the food. God tells the boy, "This is Hell." Next he brings the boy to another dining hall, same scene, people with long spoons and big bowls of food, but the difference is they are reaching across the table and feeding each other. God tells the boy, "This is Heaven."

Using power wisely is about knowing what to do to balance what goes on around us. If we kill all the bees by spraying chemicals because we do not like the look of weeds in our yard, we eventually lose an entire food chain as the bees die. Then, eventually like the hellish people with the long spoons, we will starve. Nature seems to use power wisely; it literally talks to us and tells us what it needs. Greedy people ignore the messages of the land and nature, they keep building high rises, malls, and create cities even a in desert, and then they are dumbfounded when there is no water. They are destroying nature, but nature is a wise power that does what it needs to do, in order to balance itself.

As far as balance goes, goodness and evil exist because of each other. Can you fathom that inside all of us we have the spices of sweetness and bitter in our cupboards? If there is goodness inside us and we ignore it, forget about it, lose it, then we are lost in a consciousness that can only create more weakness. Our goodness exists not just to do the right thing but also to serve us so we can be in balance. It brings us back to the table over and over to nourish us so we can feel love.

We have incarnated during a most tumultuous time on Earth when many things like weather patterns and political dynamics are threatening the world. How we create our reality in rebound to these difficult threats is the bet we are placing our power on. So can we consider ourselves as extraordinary beings that fight evil, mostly in ourselves? To stand in the face of what is dark and bring light to it is a heroic task. To be able shift our personal reality in the midst of whatever reality is upon us is another heroic task. So we work with what goes on, disagree with what is not evolved, and so we get loud about it—and we shift it! We can do that because that is what superheroes do!

Two little girls, who live in the mountains and are not glued to a computer screen, are out on a spring day playing in a field. They come upon a beautiful stick and accordingly, one child picks it up and flipping it around pretends the stick is now her magic wand. She boldly announces "Abracadabra!" and then declares a manifestation of something she wants to happen. Smiling she turns to her friend and says, "This is how it is." Her friend agrees and they continue skipping down the lane to look for more magic.

As we are whirling in motion on this magical journey, the mental wands we have been gifted with have neither discrimination nor intelligence; they just tap into our thought forms and actualize them. Our entire existence is all about an exchange of energy patterns that create, maintain, or discard storylines. Therefore nothing is haphazard, there are no hits or misses, no accidents or mistakes, as everything that exists has a force field and it is up to us how we use it. Imagine if you had a plug attached to your finger and everything around you had a socket and you were always on call to decide what to plug into, it's like that. Now imagine that you also have a socket, maybe right in your forehead, and people, things going on, and stories, are plugging into you. In a way it's like this, an exchange of energy either plugs us in, or plugs into us, so we must be aware, and determine what is allowed access to our force field.

When we have a motive, our consciousness bands together like the moods of The Seven Dwarves, singing, *"Hi-Ho Hi-Ho it's off to work we go."* As we gather all the aspects we are dealing with into a proposed influence, all the moods and stories are put down. Alternatively, our consciousness is in conversation with the earth and beyond this: the universe. The universe is not an audience in a comedy club and cannot decipher if we are goofing around when we jokingly say things like, "I'm broke, it's killing me, people never come through, and I'm F—ked." As we speak, atoms and molecules are lining up, geared to manifest these very words. If we continue to talk about what a pain in the ass it all is then we should make sure our medicine cabinet is stocked with Preparation H, as serious hemorrhoids are in order. If you want to spend your day at the mall driving around in circles, keep affirming how crowded it is and how there are no parking spots. You never get a good seat at the movie, a table in the restaurant, there are no taxis at rush hour, the house isn't selling, your husband is cheating, and your boss is two-faced. Maybe it's all-true, but the question is how do you fit into the truth of it?

Our words are our magic wands: "It's too hard, it won't work, I'm exhausted, they're always late, they've cheated me, I have no money", on and on it goes. A friend who was writing a book kept calling it the damn book, she always had to go work on the damn book, I told her to call it the gift as who wants to read a damned book.

Hello in there, it's your call. While you were not conscious, your distorted mind was online placing orders to arrive with overnight delivery. If our unconscious mind is busy affecting our atmosphere, then our conscious mind must clean up the aftereffects. So whatever is going on, decide how to see it; when we see the delays, the confusion, and all the actual blockages as alternate routes, we are seeing that we either need to go another way, or go into time out and wait for the wind to change. In yoga after difficult postures we always go into a child's pose where we rest and take a few breaths and then start again. Time out is the same, it's equivalent to being pulled back like an arrow in a bow, this is the time to let go and relax because magic is happening.

In actuality, perhaps today your bank account is low, your husband is looking at his secretary with lustful eyes, you can't get the reservation you want at your favorite restaurant, it took a while to park, your best friend was talking behind your back, it was a hard bad day and nothing went well. Maybe worse things than that happened and you wonder how you could have created any of this. How could you control a table opening at a restaurant, or your husband's roving eye, or even worse things? We can't control those things, it's not the actual situation we must control; it's the energy around things and how it affects us.

Stop the negative babble and say the opposite, even if you don't believe it. The goal is to shift, so evaluate the unwelcome causes and effects: the motivations, the origins, and the principals of the elements you are dealing with. Many of the low-level things we believe are not good enough to invest in. Every single thought has an alternative thought cycling around it, choose the one with the highest intentions. If there is no table at the restaurant try believing that the universe wanted you to find a fabulous new chef, or maybe there was someone special to meet at the next restaurant down the road, this is how we attract magic. By constantly upholding our state, even on the less important stuff, then when the big serious stuff rolls in we are well trained.

Consider that life is creation in motion and we are energetically spinning like whirling dervishes on a planet that is also spinning. Then acknowledge that there is a pivotal power point somewhere and the goal is to find it, stand in it, breathe in it, eat in it, fall in love in it, and live in it. You would think this would be easy but we are bombarded with non-stop dynamics that are geared to deter us. We don't know upfront how sometimes we are delivered gently into a comfort zone or why at other times our bus breaks down and we are dumped off at the distraught cafe. Either way we need to be cool around all atmospheric settings and know that we are just passing through. Empowered from a heart-felt genuineness, we take the best and leave our best, as this is how we affect a collective consciousness of general beliefs. We are like a living human purification system that uses our existence as an offering to create a small shift wherever we go.

I read about an upscale Manhattan hairstylist who went out every Sunday to find homeless people on the street and cut their hair. He felt a need to give strangers a way to feel better. One homeless fellow looked in the mirror after his haircut and said he would now go get a job. No matter what we do for a living, we all have a way to give back.

I was given too much change at the grocery store and did not realize it until I was many blocks away. Passing a Laundromat, I saw a mother with four children, doing loads of another family's laundry. I took her children next door for ice cream, granted they loved it, but the gift was mine. Every time we give, we are gifting ourselves. The girds of the universe are connections that restore the universal lines constantly to remove the static. In the same way that our actions of goodness restore and reset our karma, one good action overrides a bad one. When there is an abundance of goodness in our accounts, the miracle lines are open.

I once reached out to a very powerful healer via email and asked them to balance out something I was having trouble with. I felt a shift immediately after I hit send. I never heard back from that healer but I have a feeling that their higher self got the message and just fixed my issue. So how far-fetched is it that someone's higher self could do a healing on us, or crossing paths with a turtle could give us an insight, or being caught in a rainstorm could be a cleansing? When we are sensitive and in conversation with all that exists, we know that everything has a broadcast system that is speaking to us. Messages, energy, and miracles, come through when the lines are clear.

A friend visiting me was sharing her pain over her inability to get pregnant. I put my hands on her and asked the universe if it was for her highest good, to please clear the energy that was blocking this ability for her. Suddenly two young does appeared in my yard and my friend said by seeing them, she knew she would have two children. She asked me what I did and I said, "Personally I did nothing, I just asked the universe to help you." She conceived a month later.

Crazy things happen that don't make sense to our adult minds, but since we are re-mixing our programs, consider consciously giving your esoteric mind free-range. This part of the mind has a psychic division that contains impulses, images, and ideas. Here, we connect with the phenomenon that is beyond this physical world. We connect with extraordinary impressions that come from far away, even other dimensions, and these impressions have the power to help us, protect us, and open our treasury of genius. We can

ABRACADABRA

tap into this magical vortex and channel its divine healing energy into our own beings. On the one hand this is a big deal, and on the other hand, it's just a normal extraordinary experience.

Our great power lies in knowing what is extraordinary, and when you think about it, most things are. Consider a near death experience, someone very close to me left this world and came back. This experience hosted a heightened awareness that makes no sense here, but really it made perfect sense to my friend. They were aware that they had left this world but were still alive somewhere else and in conversation with another version of themselves. Leaving this world and coming back to life is quite stunning but was most spectacular was the fact that they were basically aware that they existed in more than one dimension. This certainly changes one's perspective and removes the, this-is-all-there-is, concept."

We are our own healers. We are our own everything: from mothers, to art directors, to gurus, to warriors, to maid service, to spiritual advisors. We are powerful designers of our own montages, which can be constantly altered since our diversity shifts, as our options become viable. As we gain knowledge, everything continually changes, because we keep progressing from our new wisdom. Since we are our own guru, a word which means from darkness to light, we must align only with the beliefs that hold substance, the ones we can grow from, the beliefs that will carry us when we stumble. A friend commented that, "It's easy to be spiritual

170

when everything is going well, but to still be spiritual when everything has gone to Hell is genuine spirituality."

How do we hold onto our most powerful state? Imagine floating down a river filled with thousands of fish, each one is a thought and they are jumping out of the water all over the place. You're there with your fishing pole and net catching tons of them, they're filling your boat so fast that you are starting to sink. Now you will have to start throwing some back, so you throw back the small ones that are not good enough. There are still too many so you need to make a decision; are you going to keep just what you really need or are you going to be greedy and go down because you are overloaded?

The portrayed river is akin to our mind's mental stream of consciousness, which is a continual incessant torrent of hypothesizing opinions, judgments, warnings, and desires. Amidst our mind chatter there is also the nourishing food that will sustain and fuel us. To recharge we must throw back the thoughts we don't need and expand on the ones that enrich us. This is how we hold the most powerful state.

Playing with our power is part of our great experiment in learning how to use it. Yes, getting in front of someone might give us a better position but it does not give us power. Actually there is more power in standing back, being in the worst position and being fine. Not unlike children watching the flame, we want to touch everything, as this is how we learn. Our most potent lessons come from the outcomes of our own actions—the chain reactions that set the sequels.

Going out of our zone is fun, as when we travel we are no longer who we were because no one knows our story. Our treks off into the wild are a reset in the sense that there is no familiar story; each footprint is a new story. We step off the line, we come back, it's a dance we do with our soul. Being in balance is knowing how far out to go, because some of us go too far and don't come back. In yoga when we go too far we hurt ourselves, in life the consequences of going too far can be so dangerous that we may actually leave this world. On the other hand holding back is a jail sentence so fling yourself out there but be in balance as you do it.

Magical wisdom is way beyond strategic maneuvers, it's about stepping into union with what moves our hearts and takes us across all boundaries to our promised land. Why would we ever hold ourselves back from there? Is it fear, or lack of funds, or because what we want seems to make no sense? The answer is usually yes, yet none of these reasons are good enough to block us. When we push ourselves out there, we are available to be grabbed by our spirit, and magical things happen. Imagine standing on the highway of your dreams with your thumb out? All I can say is get to that highway and get your thumb out, the rest is magic.

To define our true power, we must come to comprehend the concept of *a fortiori*, a Latin term, which means: for a stronger reason and with certainty. Our certainty resides in tapping us into the whirlwind of our innermost dervish. Even as other concepts circle around us in trying to dissuade us, it is our assurance that dispels our doubts. In the moments we are drawn into our certainty we are beyond right or wrong, beyond any other considerations, we are just grabbed by conviction and this is our truth. When we follow it, we are led to our power place. In a state of inner certainty we are in our holy land and nothing else matters. Do we sacrifice for that? Hell Yes! Sometimes when we leave our proposed security, we have nothing, we are standing out-of-bounds in the bliss of our certainty and this is enough.

Imagine finding your power place in every thought and way of being, every destination, and arrival. If you can't find it or you feel it doesn't exist, then create it. Consider going on a quest to the beach, or even on a walk, and you are questing to reset your energetic balance, as your intention is to calibrate your mind, body, and spirit. Here, the power is not in the action but in the intention, which can happen anywhere and simply takes a thought. Other times the power is in the action, or even in the act of not acting. To discern where the power is, is to know where we are. To know where we are, is instant awareness of where the power is and if we are in sync with it.

Our true power does not parade down the street but is quietly sitting on a park bench looking at the stars. It strides in a leap of faith, an honest tear, and a turn-around pirouette on a stuck thought. It moves in the realization that we have to do something or nothing; it moves like the wind and teaches us to never stay the same. Our true power is not in the payback generated from who's right, a corporation, being skinny, a luxury car, jewelry, an expensive pocketbook, being a movie star, doing the most awesome yoga postures, religions, the government, your lover, or little green pieces of paper called money. Our power is in what is personal to our heart, maybe studying the beauty of a flower, playing with a dog, inventing a new creation, running our business, dreaming a new dream and being totally immersed in our divine *fortiori*.

I was at a Patti Smith Concert. It was an acoustic set in a small theatre. She was just warming up and getting in tune when a man yelled out from the audience, "Turn it up!"

Patti jokingly said, "I feel bad."

Another fan shouted, "Don't feel bad, Patti!"

Patti then said, "I don't really feel bad, there ain't no man that can make me feel bad."

The audience went nuts because she actually did not turn up the sound; she turned up her juice and used her energy where it belonged—in her power.

It's time to hang out at the empowerment café and order a double dose of certainty with an instant refill of self-confidence. All the people around us might think we are crazy and all that matters is that we are crazy good with ourselves. What is special is not how important we are, but how our love manifests itself in how we feel about ourselves. Rodney Yee jokingly spoke one morning in yoga class of his struggles with himself to show we all have them. He then said, that when he died, maybe his beautiful wife would put *"He Breathed With Grace"* on his tombstone. How poignant, I thought to even breathe with grace. In yoga, the breath is a power place; it's our life force and by using our breath we recharge ourselves. Using the breath as a conscious vitality is to move energy through our beings. The breath as energy may fulfill a specific desired purpose, possibly towards an enlightened thought, a cleansing, a heart opening, or to just anchor us back into our source. In yoga class we are continually breathing in odd ways, always watching the breath. The breath is a guide for where we hold back and don't flow, it shows us where we are out of balance.

Rodney is constantly changing the breathing patterns for different postures; he says the breath is the power of the posture. In a crisis we are always told to breathe. When women give birth, we use our breath to push the new life through. The first thing we do when we arrive here is to take that first potent breath. We enter the world and gasp for that first breath of life force. Try to remember how potent that first breath was; imagine how serene your last breath might be. Being conscious of our breath is being conscious of how we live. Is it shallow, is it rapid, is it a struggle, does it fuel us? Our breath is our interaction with the world, our mind is the playing field and our heart is the destination.

An experiment was done at Stanford University on the behavior of baboons. It was found that after spending only three hours a day foraging for food and six hours sleeping, the remaining hours of baboon time were spent annoying and harassing each other. Instead of playing with toys they were playing with each other's minds. Why would they want to stress each other out? They were vying for the power to rule the roost, but the funny thing is that it's all still monkey business.

We cannot control, calculate, and manipulate energy from the outside; it's just another illusion that we just get lost in. External sources will not supply the qualities of power that one searches for in other people, places, and things. These are all distractions. One cannot really respect themselves without holding the same consideration for others. Our relationships and how they exist define where we stand on the barometer of self-respect. Can we respect a cheater, a liar, a manipulator, and a selfish person? The real question is can we still respect someone who is lost and let that be? Big question!

The greatest consideration is about stepping beyond the lower intricacies of what people do in their weakness. The concept is about if can we rise above low-level demeanors and still honor what goodness exists, even if it only exists on our side of the coin. The act of being empowered is about being able to hold a greater state than what is on the table. Empowerment is our energetic wealth, which warrants personal victory. Our victory is not about charging in from the front or pushing from behind. We show up replete with gifts to share, the gifts unfold with no holds barred and a disturbance is neutralized. As such we have no desire to jest with the activities of a prize-fight, armed aggression, or everyday feuding. Even though some people consider a good brawl a sport, people express pleasure when think they've won; I wonder what they have won besides false power? Real power doesn't reside in these interactions. Real power lets go and moves away when there is nothing evolved to lift off from.

Sex is a potent transference of energy between beings; it is a portal for human creation, a force field of love, and a sublime surrender into divinity. Without the wisdom to use this power wisely, it becomes a way to use others for self-pleasure. People use sex for power in the same ways they take energy from each other; it eventually expends more energy. When two people become physically intimate, their spirits enmesh and in our new fast-track culture we tend to treat this casually. It needs to be recognized that when we're dressed and on our way, there is a subtle body of our personal energy that we have left behind that it is now being held by the warm someone we've just slept with. It's funny that we call it sleeping together, an act we do while not awake, as opposed to making love. This is not a casual act and to treat is as such slams the door on our true passion.

The body, mind, and spirit of true love is a parade of energy where even when you do not know the cause, as the parade sweeps by, you are lifted in spirit with it. A charged energy field can do that; it can literally move you back to who you are in spirit. An energy field moves like a wave in motion and depending how our personal energy field intertwines with it, is how graceful our movements around our personal power are. When a huge wind of negative energy comes towards us, we can interact by assisting it in its passing. If we push against this kind of an energy field we give up precious personal fuel, lose our balance and fall. When we have a strong foundation, we can move in all directions with energy because we know we are coming back to our core. To be in the flow, release the mind out of the way and move into motion by feeling the energy stream—it will lead you to move with it.

All that matters is that our life force is active, our energy flow is moving and we are moving with it. As we interact with the energy fields, we have to be sensitive or energy will bang into us, knock us over, and drag us down a wrong street. I once had an argument with a friend I was doing business with who decided she was now boss. I told her my thoughts about that in a heated moment when the place of power would have been for me just know who she was and let it go. I wished I'd never gone there because it was not worth dealing with the bad feelings afterwards. My peace was broken and I broke it.

The ego wants to win and runs out into on going traffic with a sword, while our spirits shake their heads at our silly participation in these jousts. The exhilarating charge we momentarily feel in an ego related endeavor is actually the rush of energy that is moving quickly as it leaves us. In a power struggle, which all wars are, both parties are stuck in a Hell zone and there is really no winning. We are in training to sit still when our discomfort makes us want to go into our bull-on-fire mode; we must wait until we are calm to act. When we get all charged up, to enhance the charge is immediate failure.

I was caught in the midst of a backstabbing business transaction; it was complete with cheaters and covert activity. It had a charge that grabbed me and I started to go right into my normal routine of getting my ammunition lined up for battle. While planning my strategizing and gearing up for warfare, I absentmindedly picked up the fortune cookie from the previous night's dinner that was sitting on the dining room table, which I was circling like a hawk. Opening it and reading the fortune, I stopped dead in my tracks and smiled as I realized I don't get away with anything these days. The fortune cookie said: *"He who controls others may be powerful, but he who has mastered himself is mightier still."*

The secret to quickly finding the power position is to look for where there is resistance. Resistance is the gatekeeper of the ego. The moment you come face to face with a defensive mode, your goal should be to quickly drop back and let it go, it's instant relief. So set your alarms to go off the moment you feel falsely fueled, the moment your heart turns to stone, the moment negative words dribble out of your mouth. Watching yourself is an act of self-consideration—controlling yourself is an act of mastery.

If you are not on a quest for what is extraordinary you will be lost in the land of ordinary and not see the magic. "Quest" is the root of the word *question*, which means to explore, discover, inquire, and seek out. Our quest is in looking beyond where we are for a solution to the answers, to find our solace in an alternative experience. Our treasures are out there going one way, while looking deep within for them is the way to find them. On these expeditions for treasure many times the endowment is hidden in the most obvious places, in fact many times it is so obvious that we don't see it.

One morning during a difficult yoga posture Rodney said, "To relax in the ordinary, is to find the extraordinary." This opened my mind to consider a state of relaxation in a power struggle, a sigh of relief in a time out, even a moment of peace in a war zone. To relax is liberation. Knowing that there is magic in what is ordinary is to see the familiar in a new way. This great expanse of magic loosens our concepts of what is possible; it loosens all our stuff and delivers us into the amplification of the highest essence that exists in all things.

The Hindi word, Namaste' means "I offer the highest salutations to you." This word honors with reverence what is the highest form of being in another. How often do we kneel in our heart to the embodiment of worshiping what is good, what is dharmic, what empowers us with right action? Salutations to us for coming here and doing the best we can. Salutations to us that we are awakened to becoming the conductor of our own evolved consciousness. Salutations to the highest aspects of our beings, may we walk forward holding hands with the highest essence of our selves. With great respect and with great love we must welcome the highest in ourselves with all our heart and gently let go of the rest.

Atma Prema is another Sanskrit word for self-love. The atma is considered the higher self and prem is a concept of elevated love. As we come through the mire of loving ourselves through failure, through misfortune, through all the hard times and pain, we stand on the other side of it all. To go beyond conceit and vanity to the core of our well-being is where the supreme advantage exists. The elevated genre of our prosperity is abound in wise action—this is our true power. We are great beings who must find our treasures and share them. Granted some of us have gotten lost and have therefore turned away from the best of who we are. Can we look at these people and be even more grateful that we did not lose ourselves this way, or even if we have, that we are in the process of coming back. As heroes we will live with the consequences of sharing space with lost beings and we will clean up their mess and send love to their relatives. We do it because in order to set ourselves free from suffering, we do something about it.

In Buddhism there is a meditation that cuts the roots of suffering and it is not for the fainthearted. It's about dissecting to the marrow exactly what our suffering is about by observing if it's unchanging and functional and to finally challenge it, to see if it's true. Our existence is naturally geared to bring kindness and peace into all our migrations. In our most powerful state, our footprints, our movements, and our words are all a dance done in harmony. We move lightly and gently with absolute power and we support each other. When we are complete within ourselves we are no longer hungry for power, we are full—Powerful!

Reflection:

Imagine the feeling of having a full cup; having vital life force charged with a dynamic energy field where all that is needed, easily comes to be. Own that feeling and store it. Now imagine the opposite we have nothing, we are struggling, nothing works, and we are exhausted and sick of it all. Now pull back up the first dynamic feeling and impose it into the second suffering. Just in the fact that you held onto that first good feeling means it's in there to be tapped into when you need it. Now, let the first feeling override the second feeling of hopelessness, commit to continuing to spark that first good feeling. Let the second hopeless belief fall apart as the first feeling colors it like food dye falling into water.

On this journey of highs and lows we must be the captains of our ship. Since this life is like the high seas, there is no time for games of thievery with others; we have to be one with our vessel to stay afloat. We enjoy the peaceful calm days and bask in them so when the storms roll in we have the strength to hold on. Many times on our great adventure, we are called to a meeting of the minds with who we are in spirit; we commune with the Gods of our dreams for sustenance and honor the universe for her compass guide and great messages to aid us. We fathom that we are not in this dance alone, that we arrived empowered to use all that we have to stay afoot until it is time to lay ourselves down with a smile on our face no matter what. So we move on and we hold onto the smile, we remember this smile in each instance we collide with, and we use it to mark the line of our outcomes. The question and the challenges become about what it will take for us to walk away with this great smile. And whatever it takes is what we do because this is where our great power lives.

So maybe in the beginning we had to put on the guise that we were OK to get by, but now we are free of external manipulations, because by our own hand we are full and nourished inside. The seal of our own approval is a magnificent power wand that makes us smile as it transforms all that we are, have, and do, into the dream of who we are in our full power as we beam with our own delight.

PS. We don't have to pretend anymore.

The Miracle Zone
Our Magic

"We are the miracle of force and matter—
making itself over into imagination and will.
Incredible.
The Life Force experimenting with forms.
You for one. Me for another.
The Universe has shouted itself alive.
We are one of the shouts."
—Ray Bradbury

Everyday the universe is talking to us, offering us an opportunity and challenging us to break an old spell to step into our wizardry. We have days where everything goes wrong, our perception goes out of focus, our emotions go haywire, our higher state has left the house as we are left sitting on the edge of our comfort zone—helpless. The mantra I repeat when I feel my magic has deserted me is: *"I request to be present in the Miracle Zone!"* This zone bypasses all actualities and calls forth the apex of how I dream to exist in this actual Earth dimension. Personally, I don't want to just survive—I want to be astonished!

This first mantra opens the door and my next mantra is: *"I Am Now Present in the Miracle Zone!"* We are, as we believe, we just need to get ourselves there.

Albert Einstein said, "There are two ways to live: you can live as if nothing is a miracle; or you can live as if everything is a miracle." Even the word *Miracle* itself has a potent energy field. Miracles are attached to a vital magical force that comes from beyond this world, bringing with it extraordinary happenings that bypass all reasoning. A miracle will create activity that is well beyond any natural law, for when a divine force comes through and takes over, it has supernatural causes that can be considered a *Force of God, a Universal Force, or a Cosmic Blessing;* such happenings are all beyond the powers of man. Accordingly, our existence is also a miracle as we all arrived from another dimension escorted by a supernatural force that had the power to create us. So if we came from miracles it is our responsibility to support their existence and serve on their production team.

The miracle zone has created great wonders of the world, like: The *Great Pyramid of Giza, Stonehenge,* the *Taj Mahal, Findhorn,* and many other sacred places that are not even known. You could open a portal to a miracle zone in your house, your car, or an aisle in the supermarket by holding a miraculous thought. A miracle zone is opened by invitation, by a circumstance that calls for it, by destiny. To arrive in a miracle zone calls for a shift in consciousness. To state that a miracle zone exists is the first step into the shift. The second step is to know that we are surrounded by the magic of miracles, and thirdly, to begin to see them and use them.

In the opposite sense of negative thoughts, bad days, and experiences that seem as far-removed from a miracle as possible; if we unjustified these kind of experiences as not the priority of our expectations, then we are still holding the door open for elevated possibilities to arrive. We are like the doorman to our own private event discerning who gets the VIP pass. Granted at a good party, invitation only is what makes it special. Our life experience is the same, as we must discern what gets in. What makes things special is how we see them, consider a simple rock, it's either just a rock or a conglomeration of earth that holds ancient energy. Imagine seeing things the way your cat or dog sees them, what level they look at things from, and how is it possible they have such unconditional love? It's all a matter of consciousness, so now consider losing your mind and creating a new one from scratch. If all the experiences that solidified all the patterns of our behavior were deleted, we would be free to be closer to who we are in spirit. Thus being a free wondrous being with no holds barred. Living like this is miraculous.

By thinking about things in an esoteric manner we are tapping into a magical grid of what may be rendered possible and therefore empowered with the energy to bring our ideas into existence. I think of the magical grids as if they were a ladder that you can crawl along sideways on into another dimension. So as things are going on in one realm, it is possible to go into another realm and do something else. Granted that the universe does not often make sense, so we have to make our own, and the farther from sense we go the more magical things become. We are just reaching into the beyond, grabbing a miracle from there and releasing it here. How it then manifests itself is its business.

Magical grids are real and exist everywhere from in our minds, to along the lines of the actual earth map, into outer space and beyond. Earth grids form a matrix of geometric patterns called Sacred Geometry. These patterns have potent energetic dynamics that bring healing, enhance energy fields, and open the portals into other dimensions. Ley lines are the pathways and channel alignments that connect the energy grids that run across the planet. Like phone lines they also tap into zones that channel miraculous energy into the Earth's field. Different sacred geometric symbols hold divine energy and can be used for clearing, protection, and balancing harmonious energy into an area.

An octahedron, a four-sided pyramid with six points, is one such power symbol. I consider this symbol a potent healing chamber as I mentally place my astral being inside it to clear my energy field when it becomes stagnant. Shapes, symbols, designs, art, and music all coerce energy. The upside down triangle of the abracadabra symbol reminds me that the miraculous magic falls from above into the lower dimensions. There is an expanse of information out there that supports this very ancient wisdom.

I tap into the sacred space of a miracle zone every time I do anything that warrants me to either step into an adventure, enhance a passion, or magnetize magic into my energy field. I never get on a plane without blessing the entire aircraft and everyone on it. I never sit on my yoga mat without asking for ethereal assistance. I never sit down to write, do a business deal, drive, eat, sleep, and even go shopping, without surrounding myself in this sacred field of magic and request to be blessed by it. We receive energy from everything that sustains us, from a meal, to a glass of water, to our breath, to the actual earth we are standing on. We also receive energy from our consciousness, which has free rein to go as far as it wants to get what it needs. Many times when I cannot get what I need around here, I know I need to journey beyond my mind and feel the sustenance I want from out there.

Perhaps a miracle is luck, a coincidence, or destiny, but really it is in the spark behind these things that makes them happen. I once had a next-door neighbor in Manhattan named Vince, whom I loved to have heart-to-heart chats with at all hours. I had gone alone on a business trip to Brazil as part of a fashion shoot crew and while in the lobby of the hotel waiting for the elevator I had a queasy moment of loneliness and fear. I was not used to traveling alone. The elevator door opened and standing there was Vince, my neighbor, looking just as shocked as I was. We both had not mentioned our traveling plans to each other and that evening at dinner together overlooking the Copacabana we acknowledged our miracle. It was God's way of telling me it's okay, your heart people will always be around wherever you go and if you don't see the ones you know then you will find new ones when you get there.

Our magic highlights its location wanting to be observed as it posts invisible communications with sign languages that speak to us in primordial symbols and dynamics. Consider two synchronistic instances bumping into each other, a perchance meeting, an un-asked for gift, a moment of grace, this is a direct contact from the hub of the miracle zone. Miracles remind us that we are so much more than we know and that we have divine support coming in from other realms.

Remember all the times you've been called forth and performed heroic acts when you really had no ability to do so? How was that possible? It was our great spirit who performed those acts. People have lifted up cars, jumped in rivers, captured thieves in the act, and run into burning buildings, to save unknown others with an otherworldly courage and strength that comes from divine realms. Most people who have performed miracles describe that they were just impelled into action, there was no choice, something extraordinary just happened that caused all the barriers to instantly fall away as the miraculous activity was performed. In the moments that we step aside of who we think we are is the moment when we really find out.

Our self-worth is sealed when we establish precedence in the fact that we have entered into a holy relationship with ourselves. This precedence makes us desire with a vengeance to move only from the positions that maintain this sacred state. Aligned with who we are in spirit, we are automatically tapped into our natural good fortune. To become captivated by our own vision is to move beyond frozen concepts, our psyche relaxes and our physical form releases endorphins, as even our muscles let go of the bone to allow us to stretch farther in our posture. When we honor this prospect of vitality as being our natural inheritance, then when it does not exist, we wait and expect its return.

Where are we going? We're going out there to co-exist in the wonderful multi-dimensional experience of our own magic. Imagine traveling into a daydream and arriving in another dimension that possibly even exists on another planet in another universe. Beyond the concept of time and the normal tick-tock of human reality, a parallel miraculous paradigm exists. We are completely fulfilled in these other dimensions, because just connecting into them from our mind's eye releases their sustenance into the here and now. Consider a homeopathic remedy, which contains a minute drop of an essence that could make us sick, but it does the opposite, it strengthens us to become immune. In the same sense, a single vision of fulfillment can change an entire dynamic of our actuality. Therefore if we are strengthening ourselves to not be affected by low-level dynamics, then we must take a magical trek into our backwoods to bring back the ingredients that will make us insusceptible. We must not be afraid to wander through we-have-no-idea-where-we-are-ville, which is a very odd place designed to worry us. We also might pass through the tunnel of we-don't-deserve-to-have-goodness; these junctures are just a bunch of mind traps. We are basically just bypassing the boundaries that repress our imaginations and restrict our happiness.

A friend had gotten very ill and when she got better, she decided that she had to create a new story about believing in herself. The hiccup was that she required others to support her new story as if her own belief was not enough. She then spent a great deal of energy explaining her new point of view when the real miracle was in the fact that she had come close to death and had gotten well. Instead of focusing on and celebrating this, she was trying to figure out how to stop it from happening again. The miracle was talking to her, but she was too busy talking to herself, so she could not hear the miracle.

A person I am very close with who was at a turning point in his life, had a near-death experience and then came back to this world. He was in the passenger seat of a convertible when a tire blew out. The car flew in the air, flipped over many times and smashed into a field by the road. He left his body the moment the car left the ground and found himself hanging out in a state of total bliss. He described being very far away and very relaxed, but as if in a dream somewhat aware of what was going on around his physical body in the crushed car. He said, he realized that if this was dying it was amazing. Suddenly he felt he had an option to come back to life and so miraculously he woke up basically undamaged except for a few bruises and cuts. Considering the state of the car, there was no reason for him to be alive. Miracles like this are life changers.

There is a fine line between the here and there. There are many people who want to believe that beyond this life existence there is nothing. I believe it to be a continuation of where our spirit travels. Either way we will all find out. I have also experienced a continuation of communications with loved ones even as they have crossed to the other side. There are really no barriers between here and there. The only barriers are the ones in our minds that separate everything. Consider that someone has left this world; nevertheless we are still always connected to them. In thinking about my late parents and the great chapters in my storyline that they were involved in, I still feel their impressions constantly, so how far gone are they really? I feel their connection in my cells, in my heart, in the history of our story together, and the story I have created from that story. They might not be in this physical reality with me but they exist as strongly as ever because they are a part of me.

The point is that the connections are all active, so in the same sense that we can travel across the world in a day going from the chaos of New York City to the serene Bergamo Alps in Italy, reality is expansive. Other times we don't need to travel farther than beyond our front door to experience the expansiveness of our connections. Imagine if you once called out for a miracle and on the other side of the planet a person who was sleeping had a dream and something in their dream responded to your calling. Remarkably, it was not an accident that in their travels they bumped into you in the most unusual place to tell you a quick little secret that held the key to your calling. Perhaps it was an angel who took your message to them knowing they were coming your way and could give you the answer you sought. It might sound a bit farfetched but when things are meant to be there are no coincidences, as when you called out a seed was planted, and from your serendipitous meeting it would bear its fruit.

Magic and Miracles have common bonds in that they are inexplicably spontaneous and wondrous and drawn to each other like the sea and the sand. When one of them arrives it is on the coattails of the other. The secret to having a magical life is to be grateful for the simple things: the switch that turns on the light, the car motor that ignites, your socks when your feet are cold, the fact you can contribute love. In our everyday existence our automatic functionality of walking, driving, or even just sitting and thinking, revolves around abilities we usually take for granted. A shift of perspective to grasp that miracles exist, makes them known, and then these miracles hold hands with our hearts, saying over and over, "I told you so!"

As a child I never got through an hour in a schoolroom without traveling out on a speck of dust to float around the room while singing heartily and loudly to myself. They said I was disruptive back then, an underachiever at school, and they wanted an explanation. What my teachers did not realize was that in the delirium of my contentment I was traveling at light speed in a sideways elevator through parallel universes right to where miracles live. As far as our daydream thought processes go, it's just unexplainable that one moment we may be sitting on a bus and then poof we're gone. It's comparable to being called to an enchanting soiree and at the same time we are still right where we are. It happens to me often at the beginning of a yoga class while sitting waiting for the class to begin, people are talking, getting props, finding spots, there is a lot of activity, I see the light coming in through the window, peace just descends over me and I feel as if I am in a multi-universe. I know it sounds crazy but as we step out of a regular 3D dimension, a captivating mystique descends to take us on its journey. When it happens to me in yoga, one minute I am stiff and can't touch my toes and the next moment I am flowing through postures. A natural spell of infused magic and fresh energy takes over.

I could have tried to explain to my teacher who was bothered by my absent mindedness in my early school years, that I was just distracted by my fascination of being in other worlds. I could have described how I floated away on a speck of dust in a light beam coming through the window, but she wouldn't know what I was talking about. If she were still around, I would just hand her the Tarot card of *The Fool,* which basically explains it all. The Fool stands alone apart from others on the edge of the cliff. A Fool always follows their own rules as they thrive on spontaneity, what is unpredictable and unexpected. They take crazy chances, trust their hearts desires, and live with joy. They are always heading into the unknown and beginning a new adventure. The Fool card has no number, it is in the zero zone, which exists between the positive and negative. So the Fool is in his or her own universe, neither here nor there. The card depicts a dog barking to call them back from the edge—back into a more solid reality, but the Fool is basically gone.

The Fool is mostly innocent with arms flung open to embrace whatever is out there. They stand in a posture of lift-off looking to the heavens, precariously on the edge of a cliff, as if in a thrust of splendor. Their load is light; actually they carry a very small satchel, as one does not need much when stepping into the dimension of infinite possibilities. The Fool's persona is a lifeline that can pull one out of conventional thinking to reveal expanding horizons.

Not everyone can understand the *Fool on the Hill*, but as the Beatle's song goes: *"And the eyes in his head, see the world spinning round."* The Fool can see way beyond this world and what he is seeing . . . spins dreams. When we let all the stories of the world just spin, we can stand back and decide which ones we want to spin with. We must allow the pain and sadness around many of these stories to spin as well, so that they don't stagnate, they just continue spinning to transform themselves. The fool stands back, watching it all from his elevated perception in a trance. He is busy reaching into infinity, so we can't expect a fool to be serious, to be organized, or to act accordingly. Fools make mistakes, they often fall down, they speak their minds, and they laugh at their own folly. We were taught to never to be the fool, forget that, now be the Fool and you will see how close to heaven a fool stands.

Reaching beyond our perceptions gives us a better understanding of each other. A fellow on my Abracadabra, Create As You Speak Facebook page, shared a dark perception in response to something I had posted that was light-filled and addressed my hopes for peace in a time of potentially another war in the Middle East. This fellow saw the opposite; actually he probably was just seeing one reality of it. I went into my truth to connect with the heart of my message and replied: *"Perceptions are so interesting and possibly the road maps of where we need to invest more or less."* I find that when I feel bad, my perception is my own road map telling me where to dig for treasure. A few days later a miracle happened and we reached a step towards amity on a war outbreak and the world breathed a sigh of relief. The Facebook fellow responded a few days later with: *"You reminded me of the profound power of choice we all have and the Response-Ability to use it productively and positively. I listened and began immediately to send my thoughts into an alignment of good feelings and positive expectations. I turned on a dime, that day."*

The turn-arounds always hold a miracle, that's why the dervishes keep spinning. They are spinning miracles for the world—their spinning is their prayer. We are invited to offer our prayers to be heard in the ethers of the universe and from these prayers we are clearly stating that we are requesting to be present in the Miracle Zone. It is illustrious that we are alive in this great phenomenon and the more we marvel it, then the more we will know that we are not only surrounded by miracles, we are one of them!

Reflection:

By exploring an experience there is an opening for magical shifts to occur and therefor for miracles to arrive. To define an experience puts it in a box and shuts the lid. In times of dismay we must ask ourselves if we can advance from this experience without judging the pain factor. The answer in itself is the miracle as it tells us where to go, or simply opens another perception taking us on its journey. Accordingly the dynamic of a miracle is an interaction between us and all that exists that is divine.

Abracadabra
Our Alchemy

"And above all, watch with glittering eyes
the whole world around you
because the greatest secrets are always hidden
in the most unlikely places.
Those who don't believe in magic will never find it."
—Roald Dahl

A spellbinding moment exists, put down your bags and step into it. It has been banging on the door while we were busy playing with our problems, because we now need to drop everything and run as fast as we can to our own awakening. Our magic is the bifocal of our consciousness that can read the tiny, tiny, print that maps what exists as the greater whole of this journey of our life. Our magic knows the secret of what can harvest valuable seed from bad, and the secret is that the most powerful alchemy that exists is simply goodness. So put down your bags, surrender what you think you know and let the captivating feeling of bliss-felt alchemy take over.

In the Middle Ages into the Renaissance and the Age of Discovery, alchemy was considered as the chemistry used to turn base metals into gold. It was considered a universal remedy that was also called the philosophers stone, which was thought to be able to regenerate spirituality. This kind of alchemy symbolized perfection, enlightenment, and heavenly bliss. Considered in fables and tales, it was told to be an elixir of life. In my humble opinion the conception of this potion is a transformative seed from another dimension that can be used only in the exchange of goodness. In the concept of turning lesser metals into gold lies the message that the magic of alchemy works only in the elevation of turning one form into a higher form. Therefore to try to use alchemy for selfish purposes is meaningless because it will void itself of every kind of magic.

Alchemy has a consciousness much like the Excalibur, the legendry sword of King Arthur, which was set in a stone and could only be pulled out only by someone with the right attributes—resultantly being a rightful King. Again in my humble opinion, anyone with rightful attributes is sincerely a King, or a Queen, as such majestic considerations are warranted with the magical seeds of transformation to elevate their way. If alchemy has a consciousness then it really is a consciousness that creates consciousness. In a symbolic sense, a child could pick up a rock in the park and declare it a magical stone; they would carry it with them and believe in it until the impositions of life begin to leave no further room for magic. It is time to size up the duplicity, to reclaim our child-like magic and use it for our highest good.

The sense of highest good is not about your bank account, or your love life, neither of which you can take with you when you leave this world. It is about your great state of being, how you evolve and stand in the world with compassion, and how you support the goodness in life. Can you fathom the level of consciousness it takes to wish someone that has done awful things, well? It does not mean what they have done is okay, but that in wishing them well, we are wishing for goodness. Consider that despite the fact that at times things go crazy and may seem senseless and out of control, this duplicity pushes us to find other ways to coexist between earthy and divine ways of being. If what is going on out there seems nonsensical then what is also nonsensical in our imagination and in the creation of our dreams, is valid.

A planned for experience leaves no room for magic, magic does not exist in what is known, or what is on the page, it must be read between the lines. The difference between what we maneuver and what comes to us on the tail of right action is the difference between conjuring and real alchemy. We can acomplish spend days fortune-telling, forging tricks, and getting lost in the hocus pocus of performing impossible feats, but when we reach the level to understand alchemy, we are beyond all that. When we step into who we are in our highest domain and act within the accordance of our utmost principles, virtues, and sincerity;

the seeds of transformation are ours. This kind of evolved magic is an idiosyncrasy that aligns with the constitution that is most like it, so it brings back the alchemy of more goodness.

As children we were always told to be good, this directive resonated into the notion that this was something we were not and had to make happen. We watched others as role models and we saw the dichotomy of the world in them. I loved when adults said, "Do as I say not as I do." It was a great deceptive message because we truthfully know that the power of idle words cannot really override the power of incorrect actions. To be taught that good was something outside of us, something we did not innately have and had to strive for, disempowered it in us. Consider the concept of being well, being well takes away all the connotations that one is or is not good.

We have been cheated into believing that we do not already own our goodness. The truth is we are infinitely good but not always nice. Granted, we all know that evil exists, that distortion and insanity can run rampant and that we may have touched upon some of these things at times, and when we do, we also live with the consequences. Goodness lives in caring about the fact that we might have stepped off the line and we are doing something about it, like coming back. Our goodness lives in wanting the nourishment of good will; this is the philosopher's stone, the cure-all, the Midas touch of alchemy.

Alchemy will not pick the Lotto numbers or make someone love us. It will not stop others from doing bad things, it will just give us the spark to divine what we really need so we can be entranced in what exists now and work with that. As we are divining our future, we still might experience nixing feelings while visioning our dreams. Suddenly the wicked witch of our old low self-esteem comes online to tell us, "Hello dearie, nice vision, too bad you are not worthy to have it." This is when the alchemy of our good will responds by showing us that an empowered vision trumps low self-esteem, to challenge something trumps giving up, and we are done not living in a magical way.

As we journey into a higher consciousness, we will experience many mysteries and be fascinated by the synchronicity of how things unfold for our highest good. As we choose the better options, we are nourishing ourselves and integrating our energy into more potent light-filled magnetic fields. So as the stories play out, we are like actors who have stepped in without scripts, we assess the situation, find a way to participate and move the story into a more elevated direction. Even when the script calls for a quick retreat, if we still leave a blessing in the act of walking away, we are affecting the parlay by wishing it well.

A friend was depressed; she was fired off a job that was just about to culminate to its fruition after a years work. She felt devastated. Discussing shifting her life, she said she had lost her passion for everything so she could not visualize connecting with any new ideas. Since we've all been there, at times like this we must remember and connect to an older feeling of happiness, a memory of once being content, and we must hold onto this feeling as a lifeline. When we can remember the beauty, the goodness, and any grace that has ever existed for us, we are then acknowledging there is balance in life. The fact is that life will always sway back into balance; this is what naturally happens. To be in the flow, we need to come into balance with anything that is balancing and this requires trust.

The goal is to get into the matrix where the personal reasoning for our existence originates. We must trust that all that is going on is a teaching, and a practice to learn from. Everything going on is triggered from the motherboard of our true source. How do we touch upon this intrinsic womb? Pablo Picasso, said, *"The meaning of life is to find your gift. The purpose of life is to give it away."*

I believe our gift is to work through what holds us back from bliss and become the example of the one who leaps off the edge of difficulties into the pool of their heart. One summer at a meditation retreat in the Catskill Mountains, I met a fellow who had been in a wheelchair most of his life. He could not move from the waist down and was in constant pain. But his face radiated total bliss. His name was Mahadev, which means Great God. He helped everyone he met and taught them to not take things so seriously. Every time I was distraught, suddenly there he was zipping up a path in his motorized wheelchair. I would tell him my tale of woe and like a magician he would turn it into a completely other tale that called for wisdom and hero-ship. He was truly a great being, because he did not have to be anything other than what he was, a man who honored every inch of life. His existence touched hundreds of people, gave them hope and showed them that bliss was always available. Mahadev was a humble unclaimed teacher, he did not preach or write books, his life was his teaching.

In the great tale of the Wizard Of Oz, by L. Frank Baum, young Dorothy had gone on a magical dream journey where she was empowered by great personal magic. Upon landing in another world she met the good witch, really an embodiment of herself, who gave her a pair of magic ruby slippers to walk in her power, on the path back to her real home. Along the way she had to confront her dark side, the wicked witch and the flying monkeys, and of course they wanted to steal the shoes to empower their darker aspects. Dorothy seemed to be naïve, so first she had to attain the wisdom to not misuse the power in the shoes that she did not even totally understand existed. She met characters along the way that showed her how to overcome fear by seeing what was false, to bring forth her courage, to open her heart and trust herself. At the end of that dream journey she knew that she had this powerful magical prescription inlaid into her psyche all along. We all have this exact same prescription, we already have the magic—we are already there.

To a mystic being in the present moment could be about traveling into a star dimension light years away. So when we come home to wherever our sacred place is and sit in our tribal dream zone, we might all of the sudden get a crazy good message, it's a scintillating spark of insight. Our magic is always talking to us and the only way to translate the information is to first honor the message as a memorandum from our own divine source, and then contemplate what this mean for us. To fully decode this magical memorandum we must follow it by going where it leads even if we had other plans. Our most potent teachings are not in the outcomes of our repetitive patterns but in the cosmic mystical moments that are so potent with power that they sweep us into them. The world is talking to us all the time; in fact the breakthrough is that we are receiving the information.

A friend, who was concerned about her weight, went to an ice cream parlor in the middle of the night when she could not sleep and bought a big triple flavored cone with all the artificial trimmings on top. Standing outside the front door of the shop, tongue moving into action, a crazy woman passed by and knocked the ice cream cone out of my friend's hand, spit on it, screamed, "sugar is the devil" and walked away. I thought it amazing that the universe got involved in this play of action to stop my friend from indulging. I also thought bravo dear friend for manifesting this great scenario with such a potent message.

Have you ever talked to a tree, kissed a flower, asked a butterfly for help; have you seen a bird that reminded you of your deceased grandmother and knew she came to send you love? Has a complete stranger ever said something to you out of the blue that was the exact key to what you were seeking? All this stuff is real, we can talk to people without speaking, communicate with animals, plants, and dreams. We can kiss and make up without words, heal, overcome and release difficulties, without even moving our body. We can play with energy fields and chains of evolved thoughts to better what we think, believe, and manifest.

What are we really doing here? We are dancing on God's great dance floor. As we do the dance of our soul, we move through the paradox of our thought forms, our psyche, our emotions, and our passion. We dance with ourselves to move through all these benchmarks of existence, to touch upon them all, knowing that nothing is stationary. We dance with ourselves to get to the pinnacle of love that exists. The late choreographer of dance, Martha Graham, said, *"Nobody cares if you can't dance well. Just get up and dance. Great dancers are great because of their passion."*

We dance with our dreams to meet our wise one who leads us to our truth. So close your eyes and look around to find your seeds that are scattered on the ground. Our seeds come from the source of what we love; our love inspires them to sprout. Our great magic is owned by the fact that there is nothing more powerful than love. So we must dance with our nonsensical dreams, swing with the unreasonable, move with abandon with our eyes closed until we realize that we are dancing with ourselves. When you open your eyes you will know that you have swirled around in the dizziness of love. If you forgot about the magnificence of swirling in wonder with arms open, then go and sit in the children's section of a park and look around, re-experience what it feels like to be lost in reveries. Remember your sacred fool's paradise and get lost in your own treasure trove. Do you recall when you've loved a stuffed animal as much as any living thing you ever knew? Try to do it again and you will be astonished to find your love still lives there. The reason why, is that behind our whole shebang we are overflowing with love and when it's released it pours itself out on all objects whether they are inanimate or otherwise.

This book is called *Abracadabra* because everyone knows that this word is a mystical incantation that charms our magic into existence. We all remember from when we were little about the poof of the rabbit popping out of the hat, the hilarity of the nonsensical, and the delight in the possibility of the essence of *Abracadabra*. Then we grew up and got a copy of *The What Is Possible–Rule Book*, I was too busy dreaming to read mine. Obviously, many others read theirs, as people are constantly telling us their perspective of what is possible. Really other perspectives are not our business unless we ask for them. Our relationships, including the ones we have with ourselves, must not dislodge us from our sparked source. This source drives us, and not always for an outcome, as sometimes it takes a century for a spark to be received. Henry David Thoreau's radical book *Walden*, hardly sold at all during his lifetime. Now it is required college reading and probably one of the most well read books in the world. So we can't worry about the outcome. What matters most is that we are in our flow, going with our rhythm and trusting that we are in the right place at the right time, while working with what is there.

Martha Graham said, *"No artist is ahead of his time. He is his time; it is just that others are behind the times."* Our devotion to the divinity of the universe and our connection to our passion is what will save us, heal us, and make us want to dance.

A friend who was once lost in a whirlpool of grief and drugs, fell in love with a holy being in India named Neem Karoli Baba, who is no longer walking in physical form on this planet. My friend, whose name is Krishna Das, travels around the world and chants the words of divine grace his teacher inspired in him. Really he just sits on a stage and goes ecstatic with love for his teacher, he sings with reverence to his Maharajji, who was also known as the Miracle Saint. Krishna Das has the same devotion that Rumi, the great poet Saint had for his beloved teacher Shams. When Krishna Das chants, a spark of his devoted love is transmitted. People come from all walks of life to sit and chant with him, it's not about religion, its simply about love and sharing it.

Imagine if when asked what you do for a living, you could answer, "I share love." Our love is our relationship to what is divine for us and just to touch upon this is to share it. Writing this Abracadabra book always pulled me back to my source because that is where my spark exists. This book is for free-style beings that can break away from formulas because they know their heart's message is the only formula they can live from. I have revised this book and in the revision, the magic of its message was what I needed to revisit in the hundred or so re-reads. This book morphed into an entirely new book and even if the rule was: "You cant' write the same book over." Well I did. So the new rule is to follow your heart and do what you need to do no matter how radical. Really the only rules we must follow are our own, we are responsible for our beliefs, our reality, our destiny, and our unfolding. We are responsible for how we honor the goodness of this sacred incarnation and what we do with this goodness.

The only balance that matters is our own and how we move across the great horizons of the stories we come upon. How do we touch upon them, uplift them, and transform them? We offer peace around hatred, and healing around grief, and we dive into compassion because we are beings of love. Some of us have the strength to look directly at what is hideous, while others must look away; we do the best that we can. Our individual nature has seasons, our great expectations bloom in the spring of youth, while our enlightened purpose flourishes when our inner elder can be still. Our inner stillness has great oracles; let them vision your crazy good secrets. Their authority is your prophecy where your enchantments are.

So be the fool and leap into the wind of your dreams, be everything you imagine, wear all the hats, and be the alchemist who will transform your life into gold—we really can do that. We hold the philosophers stone, the substance that transmutes all chemistry. We are being called to regenerate ourselves, so dream of goodness, dream of peace and freedom, dream of relief from pain and suffering, dream of love and happiness. These dreams will manifest their magic into reality!

P.S. Many Blessings on your Magical Journey!

Acknowledgments

Endless gratitude for my adored husband Joe Barbaria. You are wind behind my sails, my best saint, and the love of my life, my best friend, and the man of my dreams.

I kiss the ground for my son Max Barbaria, a visionary. And I kiss the ground for the love of his life, Suzanne Diaz, you complete my family—I love you dearly.

Robert Schnur, my brother who has a huge heart of gold, thank you for teaching me about the flow of abundance and for being one of my best friends in this world. Love you Soumaya Schnur and thank you for the Abracadabra Infinity symbol, and blessings to Kenza Schnur because family rules.

Thank you Darlene Barbaria of Barsky Design Studio for designing this beautiful book cover. You are a spark of creativity with an overflowing heart. Cover art © nikifiva/ Shutterstock © Vector Illustration/ Shutterstock.

Thank you to all my friends, known and unknown. Karen Rosen, Lisa Olsen, Taryn Copeland, all of the grammar sisters and word sculptors who helped me.

Thank you Jason G. Anderson at Polgarus Studio for setting up my E Book and making it a magical experience.

Endless gratitude to my many teachers: Swami Chidvilasanda, Paramahansa Yogananda, Rodney Yee, Colleen Saidman Yee, Heidi, Leah, Kari, Kelly Morris, all my yoga teachers, all the healers of this world, all the great writers who have taken us on their journeys & thank you to all the great beings who have lived their dream.